The Lucent Library of Historical Eras

Leisure Life of the Ancient Greeks

Don Nardo

LUCENT
BOOKS®

THOMSON

GALE

San Diego • Detroit • New York • San Francisco • Cleveland • New Haven, Conn. • Waterville, Maine • London • Munich

For more information, contact
Lucent Books
27500 Drake Rd.
Farmington Hills, MI 48331-3535
Or you can visit our Internet site at http://www.gale.com

LIBRARY OF CONGRESS CATALOGING-IN-PUBLICATION DATA

Nardo, Don, 1947–
  Leisure life of the ancient Greeks / by Don Nardo.
    p. cm. — (The Lucent library of historical eras. Ancient Greece)
  Includes bibliographical references.
ISBN 1-59018-528-5
  1. Arts, Greek—Juvenile literature. 2. Leisure—Greece—History—To 1500—Juvenile literature. I. Title. II. Series.
  NX448.5.N37 2004
  700'.938--dc22
                                      2004006304

Contents

Foreword

Looking back from the vantage point of the present, history can be viewed as a myriad of intertwining roads paved by human events. Some paths stand out—broad highways whose mileposts, even from a distance of centuries, are clear. The events that propelled the rise to power of Germany's Third Reich, its role in World War II, and its eventual demise, for example, are well defined and documented.

Other roads are less distinct, their route sometimes hidden from view. Modern legislatures may have developed from old tribal councils, for example, but the links between them are indistinct in places, open to discussion and interpretation.

The architecture of civilization—law, religion, art, science, and government—as well as the more everyday aspects of our culture—what we eat, what we wear—all developed along the historical roads and byways. In that progression can be traced every facet of modern life.

A broad look back along these roads reveals that many paths—though of vastly different character—seem to converge at a few critical junctions. These intersections are those great historical eras that echo over the long, steady course of human history, extending beyond the past and into the present.

These epic periods of time are the focus of Lucent's Library of Historical Eras. They shine through the mists of history like beacons, illuminated by a burst of creativity that propels events forward—so bright that we, from thousands of years away, can clearly see the chain of events leading to the present.

Each Lucent Library of Historical Eras consists of a set of books that highlight various aspects of these major eras. For example, the Elizabethan England library features volumes on Queen Elizabeth I and her court, Elizabethan theater, the great playwrights, and everyday life in Elizabethan London.

The mini-library approach allows for the division of each era into its most significant and most interesting parts and the exploration of those parts in depth. Also, social and cultural trends as well as illustrative documents and eyewitness accounts can be prominently featured in individual volumes.

Lucent's Library of Historical Eras presents a wealth of information to young readers. The lively narrative, fully documented primary and secondary source quotations, maps, photographs, sidebars, and annotated bibliographies serve as launching points for class discussion and further research.

In studying the great historical eras, students also develop a better understanding of our own times. What we learn from the past and how we apply it in the present may shape the future and may determine whether our era will be a guiding light to those traveling future roads.

Introduction

From Ideal to Real: Evolving Views of Greek Culture

The influence and imitation of ancient Greek arts and leisure life remain strong throughout the Western (European-based) world. Greek temple architecture, with its rows of columns and sloping roof with triangular gables at the ends, is perhaps the most familiar manifestation of this influence. Banks and government buildings in England, Germany, Italy, the United States, and elsewhere employ this style, which is universally viewed as stately and noble. One of the more famous American examples is the magnificent structure that houses the U.S. Supreme Court in Washington, D.C. Likewise, Greek sculpture, particularly its marble figures of physically beautiful, ideal-looking men and women, is still widely imitated.

Some aspects of ancient Greek culture have spread well beyond the West and have infiltrated nearly every society and nation on the globe. The phenomenon of actors reciting scripted lines before an assembled audience was born in Greece in the sixth century B.C. Theater and drama spread to other peoples over the centuries. And in modern times, with the aid of advancing technology, these art forms found new and powerful outlets in movies and television. Another Greek leisure activity, track-and-field athletic competitions, culminated in a few large-scale ancient games. The most famous and prestigious were those held at Olympia (in southern Greece) every four years for some twelve hundred years. Today, nearly every country in the world eagerly takes part in the Olympic Games.

It is natural to wonder how these potent ancient Greek cultural influences came to shape Western culture and eventually to capture the imagination of the whole world. The simplest, most convenient way would be for them to have been transmitted directly, passed from one generation to another in an unbroken line from ancient times. However, this was not the case. Instead, most of Greece's rich cultural heritage was lost to the West and only later was rediscovered.

Moreover, after that momentous re-awakening, Greek art, literature, and so on were long viewed through a sort of filter that in many ways distorted them. Greek cultural styles became the ideal, in the eye of many people the products of a seemingly superior race of beings. Philhellenism—a deep admiration for and love of ancient Greek culture—became firmly imbedded in Western intellectual circles, whose members placed the study of Greek language and culture at the core of the well-rounded Western education. Only recently, in the past half century or so, has a more measured and realistic view of ancient Greece and the study of its art and culture emerged.

Greco-Roman Civilization

The story of Greece's cultural legacy to the modern world began as far back as the seventh century B.C., when the Romans, then the inhabitants of a small city-state in west-central Italy, first came into contact with the Greeks. For several centuries, the culturally backward and highly imitative Romans copied many aspects of Greek culture. (Some of this borrowing occurred indirectly. The Etruscans, who lived in the region directly north of Rome, felt Greek influences first and passed some of them on to Rome.) Later, after gaining mastery of all Italy and the lands of the western Mediterranean sphere, the Romans conquered the Greek kingdoms and city-states clustered in the eastern Mediterranean; and in this way Rome encountered Greek culture at its source, where it was undiluted and powerfully enticing.

Though they saw themselves as politically and morally superior to the Greeks, and more fit to rule, the Romans were profoundly

The imposing architecture of the U.S. Supreme Court building in Washington, D.C., was inspired by the temple architecture of the ancient Greeks.

impressed and influenced by Greek ideas, arts, and other aspects of culture. Over time, the two cultures commingled (although the Greeks largely retained their cultural identity), producing the Greco-Roman civilization that modern scholars often refer to as "classical." As long as Rome remained strong and ruled the Mediterranean world, Greek culture was bound to remain intact and influential.

However, Rome eventually declined and the Latin-speaking western portion of the Roman Empire fell to German and Celtic tribes in the fifth and sixth centuries A.D. Greece itself remained part of the eastern sector of the realm, which survived the western sector's collapse. This remaining political entity steadily mutated into the Greek-speaking Byzantine Empire, which increasingly became preoccupied with its own affairs and no longer felt any connection with the West. As a result, in the centuries that followed, Greece was largely cut off from the rest of Europe. And most Greek literary works were either lost or not circulated in medieval Europe (where few could read and write Greek anyway).

Rediscovering the Greeks

The situation began to change during Europe's Renaissance, which began in the 1300s. One of the main engines driving this major movement of art and culture in Italy and several other European lands was a resurgence of interest in the Greeks and their works. (At first, these were known only though Latin translations of Arabic versions. Unlike people in western Europe, Islamic scholars in the Near East had maintained a number of Greek works.) In 1488 the first printed copies of the *Iliad* and the *Odyssey*, the great epic poems of the Greek poet Homer, appeared in Europe. And in the century that followed, the works of the first-century A.D. Greek biographer Plutarch became widely read and influential among educated Europeans.

Despite the European intellectual fascination for ancient Greek artists and thinkers, their source, Greece itself, became even more isolated from the West when the Ottoman Turks conquered it in the late 1300s. The Turks maintained little contact with Europe, and for a long time afterward Greece remained a distant, exotic land that few Europeans saw firsthand. Meanwhile, the Turks did not care about preserving the ancient works of Greece. So the temples and other old buildings, long ago looted of most of their contents, continued to decay. The Turks also appropriated some of these buildings for their own use, further destroying them in the process. In 1458, for example, they transformed Athens's famous Parthenon temple into an Islamic mosque, and other parts of the Athenian Acropolis housed the Turkish governor's family and harem. (It was also during the Turkish occupation, in 1687 to be exact, that the Venetians, who were then at war with the Turks, bombarded the Acropolis with cannon fire and seriously damaged the Parthenon.)

Greece's inherited antiquities had fallen into a deplorable state. Yet the situation might not have been all that different even if the Turks had not overrun Greece. By this

Turkish structures can be seen within the ruins of the Parthenon in this eighteenth-century engraving. They were removed in the following century.

time, the Greeks themselves were mostly poverty-stricken peasants with little understanding of the scope and importance of their ancient heritage. Looking back on these times, a later Greek scholar wrote:

> The worst misfortune that can befall a once renowned race is to forget its ancestral virtues, to be oblivious of its own wretchedness, to neglect and be contemptuous of education. These things, it seems, prevailed after the lamentable downfall of Greece into [Turkish] enslavement.[1]

Also contributing to the suppression of Greece's heritage was the fact that the science of archaeology, the systematic excavation and study of past cultures, did not yet exist.

A Sanitized Version of Greek Culture

In the 1700s, however, European travelers began visiting Greece and returning with tales of the wonders they had seen. Among the more influential were a Scotsman, James Stuart, and an Englishman, Nicholas Revett. They published a series of books describing Greek antiquities in considerable detail. These works excited widespread interest in Greece among educated Europeans and inspired increasing numbers of adventurers and romantics to make the trip.

Ironically, the man who did the most to reawaken the world's interest in ancient Greek art and culture never actually traveled to Greece. Johann Winckelmann was a German-born scholar who became librarian and director of ancient antiquities at the Vatican in Rome. He collected and studied drawings and descriptions of Greek buildings and other antiquities and in 1764 published his *History of Ancient Art*. This and Winckelmann's other works had a tremendous effect on European intellectuals, artists, and poets. Meanwhile, his efforts to uncover and examine the remains of the Roman city of Pompeii (buried by a volcanic eruption in A.D. 79) initiated the new science of archaeology.

The manner in which Winckelmann and other Western romantics viewed ancient Greece—as the pinnacle of human genius, artistic beauty, and nobility—became the prevailing one. Typifying this ideal, sanitized perception of Greek culture are these words from the noted eighteenth-century German philosopher Johann Herder:

Johann Winckelmann's books popularized ancient Greek culture for Europeans.

In the history of mankind, Greece will eternally remain the place where mankind experienced its fairest youth and bridal beauty . . . beloved of all the Muses [ancient goddesses of the fine arts], victor in Olympia and all the other games, spirit and body together, one single flower in bloom. [2]

Some Philhellenes went so far as to claim that by reading the works of ancient Greek writers one might absorb some of their supposedly superior self-discipline, intellect, and virtue. Partly for this reason, during the 1800s the study of Greek language and culture became a fixture in most of the better secondary schools and colleges in Europe and the United States.

Meanwhile, in that same era, thanks to Winckelmann and others like him, archaeology began bringing new knowledge about ancient Greece to light. However, for a long time the potential for such excavations to reveal who the Greeks really were as a people was not fulfilled. This was because the scholarly community was made up mainly of staunch Philhellenes who at first viewed archaeology as secondary and inferior to "pure" studies of the surviving Greek texts. They wanted to preserve their cherished image of the Greeks as noble and exalted beings. As popular modern historian Charles Freeman puts it:

Archaeology threatened to bring out into the open a society of ordinary human beings. . . . The content of classical archaeology seemed designed to keep the human side of Greek life well concealed. It focused on the excavations of great buildings, predominantly temples. . . . The finds from these sites were described by scholars in meticulous detail, but as aesthetic [artistically beautiful] objects rather than human creations.[3]

Down from the Pedestal

The twentieth century witnessed a reversal of this traditional interpretation of the ancient Greeks. First, regular study of the Greek language and ancient Greek texts steadily disappeared from many European and most English and American schools. In the 1960s and 1970s in particular, educators began phasing out Greek studies in favor of multicultural studies that examine the contributions made by Asian, African, and other world cultures in addition to European ones.

More importantly, archaeologists engaged in unearthing ancient Greek civilization began studying more than just buildings and sculptures. The *context* of those artistic wonders now became as or more important than the artifacts themselves. In other words, scholars now emphasize that the Greeks did not create art simply to awe educated members of future generations, but rather for practical, political, and/or social purposes. The case of temples such as the Parthenon is a good example. In addition to being beautiful, they appeased the gods (by providing them a place to live when visiting earth) and fulfilled the political goal of advertising the wealth and power of the cities that erected them. Clearly, fear of divine wrath and political propaganda are the concerns of real, not ideal, people. A multitude of other archaeological discoveries have revealed further examples of the often practical, selfish, and ritualistic motivations behind the Greeks' artistic and cultural expression.

The result has been a more rounded and realistic portrait of the ancient Greeks and their artistic and cultural legacy to the world. Scholars and other people now see them as real people who had personal problems and limitations and made mistakes just like everyone else. Yet none of this more realistic assessment has erased their vitality and vibrancy as a people, nor their sometimes amazing talents, ingenuity, and perseverance. Armed with these attributes, the Greeks stepped onto the world's historical stage at a crucial point in Europe's development. One might say that they were in the right place at the right time to lay the foundations for Western civilization, even if they were not themselves aware they were doing so. There is no doubt that what they did and thought long ago still affects what people do and think today. Their politics, conquests, beliefs, and customs, and to a great degree their art, architecture, literature, and athletics, laid the groundwork for most of what came later in the West. Moreover, the Greeks no longer stand atop the pedestal on which the romantic imagination once placed them. And the realization that they were ordinary human beings rather then supermen makes their world-altering achievements seem all the more remarkable.

Monumental and Public Architecture

The most familiar surviving visual images of ancient Greece are its public buildings, on which the governments of various Greek states lavished much money, time, and effort. The most expensive and important were the religious temples. Of these, the Parthenon, in Athens, is the most famous. Other examples of Greek monumental (large-scale) architecture were town halls, palace-fortresses, public altars, tombs, and theaters. These were often as grand in scale and as beautifully designed and decorated as the temples. All were originally built of wood, but were eventually constructed of stone, making them sturdy and long-lasting.

Pride and Propaganda

In contrast, the Greeks' houses and other private structures were small, simple in design, fairly unadorned, and made of perishable materials that decayed rapidly. The fifth-century B.C. Athenian historian Thucydides made the following observation about Athens's arch-rival, the city-state of Sparta, which was known for its outward simplicity and lack of ostentation:

> [If Sparta] were to become deserted . . . I think that future generations would, as time passed, find it very difficult to believe that the place had really been as powerful as it was represented to be. . . . The city . . . contains no temples or monuments of great magnificence, but is simply a collection of villages . . . [so] its appearance would not come up to expectation. [4]

This remark might well have applied to Thucydides' native country of Athens or any other Greek state if their governments had not spent vast sums erecting temples and the like. (Athens was his country because the Greek city-states, no matter how small, viewed themselves as separate nations and never united into a single nation in ancient times.)

It was the monumental architecture employed mainly in public buildings, therefore, that gave a number of Greek states a look of grandeur, wealth, and importance.

Indeed, personal pride and the desire to impress the rest of Greece and the world were perhaps the primary reasons for devoting so much money and energy to such projects. In this regard, Athens was the most successful. Pericles, Athens's (and Greece's) leading statesman during the pivotal fifth century B.C., told his countrymen that their city was invincible and eternal and that the gods had chosen it above all other states. "You should fix your eyes every day on the greatness of Athens as she really is," he said, "and should fall in love with her.

This reconstruction shows the original appearance of the Erechtheum, one of the two major temples on the Acropolis dedicated to the goddess Athena.

When you realize her greatness, then reflect that what made her great was men with a spirit of adventure."[5]

One way to demonstrate that Athens was the marvel of Greece, Pericles held, was to honor Athena, the city's patron goddess, who had helped guide the Athenians to greatness. The people agreed and built a splendid complex of new temples for her on Athens's central hill, the Acropolis. These monuments were also effective propaganda—a showcase to all outsiders of Athenian imperial greatness. Pericles himself suspected that they would serve this purpose not only in his own time but also forever afterward. "Future ages will wonder at us," he declared, "as the present age wonders at us now."[6] Some five centuries later, Plutarch confirmed the truth of this statement, writing:

> There was one measure above all which at once gave the greatest pleasure to the Athenians, adorned their city and created amazement among the rest of mankind, and which is today the sole testimony that the tales of the ancient power and glory of Greece are no mere fables. By this I mean his [Pericles'] construction of temples and public buildings.[7]

Bronze Age Greek Buildings

Plutarch was speaking of public structures created in a specific historical era. However, some of Greece's public buildings were more prominent in one age than another; and all underwent changes in style over the centuries. To understand the story of these works (as well as other aspects of Greek culture), therefore, one must be familiar with the major ancient Greek eras formulated by modern scholars. In the Bronze Age (ca. 3000–1100 B.C.), the inhabitants of Greece learned to smelt and make tools, weapons, and other objects from bronze (an alloy of copper and tin). The Bronze Age was followed by the three-century-long Dark Age (ca. 1100–800 B.C.), in which writing, monumental architecture, fine arts, and other aspects of culture largely disappeared. Then came the Archaic Age (ca. 800–500 B.C.). During these years, prosperity steadily returned, along with the development of writing and literature, arts and architecture, and major athletic games. The Classical Age (ca. 500–323 B.C.) witnessed the so-called golden age, led by Athens, in which Greek arts and culture reached their height. In the era that followed, the Hellenistic Age (323–30 B.C.), several large Greek kingdoms rose and Greek culture spread into many parts of the Near East. Finally came the Roman period (30 B.C.–A.D. 476), in which Rome ruled the Greek lands.

It was during the first of these ages that monumental architecture first appeared in Greece (and in Europe in general). At the height of the Bronze Age—its last five centuries—two distinct peoples dwelled in the region. The Greek mainland was the home of the Mycenaeans, the first Greek speakers in the area. Meanwhile, a group of non-Greek speakers, the Minoans, inhabited the large island of Crete and surrounding Aegean Islands.

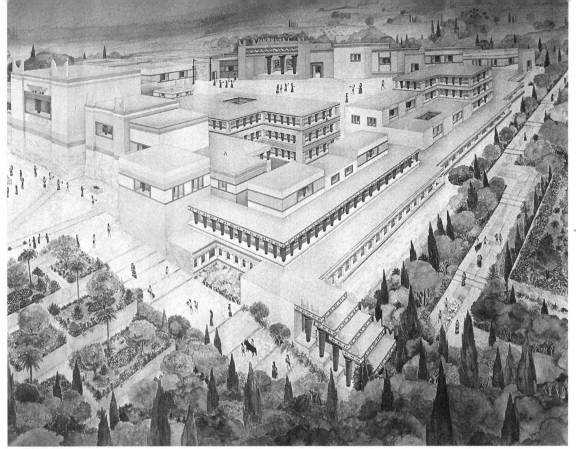

The palace-center at Knossos on the island of Crete, is reconstructed in this painting. Such centers served administrative, economic, and religious functions.

The Minoans erected several huge palace-centers on Crete. (Scholars usually call them palace-centers rather than palaces because they functioned as administrative centers as well as royal residences.) The largest and most impressive of these structures was the one at Knossos, near the island's northern coast. Excavations that began in 1900 under the direction of British archaeologist Sir Arthur Evans revealed hundreds of rooms and corridors on multiple levels. Other similar palaces were discovered elsewhere in Crete, all part of a powerful Bronze Age maritime empire. "Architecturally," the late, noted scholar Chester G. Starr wrote,

the palaces consist of mazes of rooms and living quarters organized around central courtyards and well equipped with drains and baths. . . . The staircases and other architectural details of these buildings display on an intimate scale an aesthetic [artistic] sense. . . . The major rooms were decorated with delightfully colored frescoes [paintings done on wet plaster] which depict plants and animals, real or imaginary.[8]

Unlike the rather simple, rectangular-shaped large-scale Greek buildings in the later Classical Age, the Minoan palace-centers were complex, with many winding corridors,

A Mycenaean Palace-Fortress

Here, from his book, The Legend of Odysseus, *noted scholar Peter Connolly gives a general description of the most famous of the Mycenaean palace-fortresses.*

The citadel at Mycenae was built on a hillock overlooking the Plain of Argos. Traces of at least four major roads have been found leading to the citadel identifying it as the most important center in the area and supporting Homer's claim that it was the foremost kingdom of Greece. The citadel is crowned by a palace with a great columned hall known as a megaron. The temples and the graves of the early kings are further down the slope. The citadel is surrounded by massive walls between 18 and 24 feet thick. Some of the stones are so huge that later Greeks believed that they must have been built by Cyclopes [mythical giants]. At one point the walls are still 26 feet high and may originally have been as much as 38 feet high. The main gate is known as the Lion Gate, from the two lions carved above the lintel [horizontal beam forming the gate's top]. It was defended by a bastion [fortified wall] from which missiles could be hurled at the unshielded side of any attackers. There is a similar gate in the north wall.

The "Grave Circle," lying just beyond the Lion Gate of the palace-fortress at Mycenae. Archaeologists found several royal burials in the circle.

stairwells, asymmetrical projections, and unexpected placement of rooms, doors, and windows. Another difference between the two ages was the apparent absence of free-standing Minoan temples. (In contrast, temples were *the* most prominent buildings in the Classical period.) The reason, scholars suggest, is that the Minoans worshipped at small shrines within the palace-centers as well as in caves and on mountaintops.

Meanwhile on the Greek mainland, the Greek-speaking Mycenaeans built palaces of their own. These were generally somewhat smaller than the Minoan versions as well as more fortresslike. The walls of the Mycenaean palaces were composed of huge, roughly trimmed boulders, some of them more than twenty feet thick. They were so big, in fact, that when the later Classical Greeks saw the ruins of these buildings, they thought they had been constructed by the Cyclopes, a legendary race of giants. The rooms of the Mycenaean fortresses were built around a large central hall called a *megaron*. According to archaeologist William R. Biers:

> The megaron may be defined as a free-standing unit composed of a more or less square room entered at one side through a porch with two columns and sometimes an anteroom with the same width as the main room. The principal room was dominated by a round fixed hearth, and a platform for a throne was situated against the wall opposite it. The hearth was supported by four columns, which held up the roof. Megara were

two stories high. . . . Many archaeologists believe that megara, like Cretan buildings, had flat roofs. [9]

Early Greek Temples

Eventually, the Mycenaeans, who had long been more culturally backward than and perhaps politically dominated by the Minoans, conquered the islanders. But not long afterward, the Bronze Age civilization in the region collapsed (for reasons that are still unclear). Greece then entered its Dark Age, in which no monumental architecture was produced. During these roughly three centuries, most Greeks lived in small villages, each more or less isolated from its neighbors in a valley or on an island. Over time, the settlements steadily expanded and in the Archaic Age emerged as the tiny nations that came to be known as city-states.

Religious faith and worship of the gods was an essential aspect of the societies of these small states. Each worshipped several gods but gave special devotion to its patron, a deity thought to watch over and protect the community. To make sure that the patron deity remained close by as often as possible, the people provided that god or goddess with its own house or shelter. This was the origin of the great temples whose majestic ruins still dot the Greek landscape. Because the Greeks held that the god lived from time to time in the local temple, such a building was viewed as a sacred place. Also sacred were the surrounding grounds, with the temple and grounds together constituting the god's holy sanctuary. The altars in a sanctuary were set up outside, often (but certainly not always) on the steps of the temple. (To respect the god's privacy, no worship took place inside the building, as it does in modern churches.)

The earliest of these community temples were small, simple, hutlike structures made mostly of perishable materials, including sun-dried mud-brick, wood, and thatch. As a result, none of them have survived. What have survived are a few small pottery models, including one that scholars think represents an eighth-century B.C. temple of Hera (wife of Zeus, leader of the gods). A reconstructed version of the model features a front porch with a triangular pediment (the gable formed by the slanted roof), supported by two or four thin wooden columns.

A ceramic model of an early Greek temple of the goddess Hera.

Over time, the builders of these temples extended the line of these few front columns into a full colonnade (row of columns) that stretched around the whole structure. The first-known temple erected in this style was one dedicated to Hera on the Aegean island of Samos in the early 700s B.C. In its heyday, it was about 106 feet long, 21 feet wide, and had a colonnade featuring forty-three wooden columns.

In the years that followed, the basic design of Greek temples became more or less standard. Its now familiar features included four walls forming a rectangular inner shell; a row of columns supporting a front porch, and often a back porch; colonnades running down the shell's sides; and a low-pitched roof forming a triangular pediment on each end.

Though these fundamental elements remained more or less fixed, the materials and construction methods used to erect these structures continued to evolve. For example, the roofs, which had originally been made of thick layers of thatch laid over wooden timbers, were replaced with courses of pottery roofing tiles. These tiles were extremely heavy. This meant that the underlying support timbers had to be much thicker and heavier; and in turn, the wooden columns beneath had to be thicker and stronger to hold up everything above them. For a short period during the early 600s B.C., some temples with tile roofs and wooden columns were built. One was the Temple of Apollo (god of prophecy, music, and healing) at Thermon in west-central Greece.

But with the growing desire to erect larger and more ornate temples, it rapidly became clear to the builders that wooden columns were not strong enough. Only stone versions would be able to safely carry the enormous load of the roof and entablature (the structural layer resting on the column tops and supporting the roof). By the end of the 600s, the Thermon temple's wooden columns had been replaced by stone ones; and by the middle of the following century, the changeover to all-stone temples was complete nearly everywhere in Greece.

The Doric and Ionic Orders

The seventh century B.C. was also crucial from an architectural standpoint because it witnessed the widespread adoption on the Greek mainland of an order (here meaning an architectural style) known as the Doric. With minor variations, builders repeated the standard structural elements and decorative features of the Doric order in temple after temple. The shape and execution of the columns was the most distinctive feature of the Doric style. Such columns almost always stood directly on the temple floor, without any sort of decorative base; and the top, or capital, consisted of a rounded cushion resting under a flat slab. Usually, the height of Doric columns ranged between five and seven times their width.

The Doric order possessed another distinctive structural and visual feature. Namely, its frieze, the decorative painted or sculpted band running horizontally along the entablature, was not continuous. Rather, the frieze was divided into separate rectangular ele-

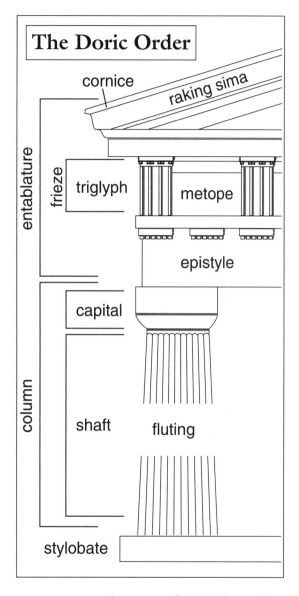

ments, or panels, some of which bore decorative sculpted figures. (Occasionally these panels were unadorned.)

While the Doric order came to dominate temples on the Greek mainland, another order, the Ionic, emerged in the Aegean Islands and in western Asia Minor (what is

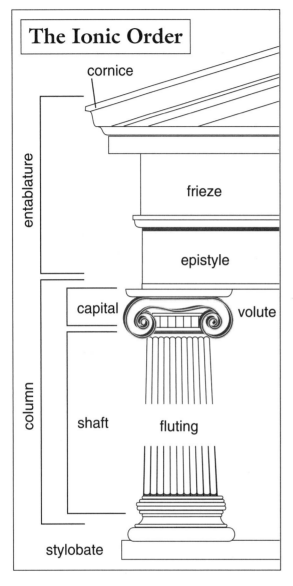

The Ionic Order

cornice

entablature

frieze

epistyle

capital — volute

column

shaft — fluting

stylobate

its frieze was usually a continuous band—rather than a series of separate panels—that ran along the entablature above the colonnade. Both the Doric and Ionic styles also came to be applied to other monumental structures besides temples, including large-scale gateways, tombs, altars, and buildings for storing treasure.

Whatever kind of building they were used for, these architectural orders were concerned mainly with aesthetic effect—that is, making a structure look well proportioned and beautiful. And over time architects came to realize that a building that was too long or too wide did not please the eye. This was especially true in the case of temples. The eighth-century Temple of Hera at Samos, for example, was five times as long as it was wide; and by the sixth century such proportions had come to be seen as ungainly and unattractive. Eventually, builders settled on what all agreed was the most balanced and pleasing ratio of length to width—roughly two to one. With few exceptions, that ratio called for six columns on each end and thirteen columns on each side (counting the corner columns twice).

A number of all-stone Doric temples utilizing this two-to-one ratio arose in mainland Greece during the sixth century B.C. One outstanding example was the Temple of Athena Polias (Athena "of the City") on the Athenian Acropolis. This building, along with other structures on the Acropolis, was destroyed in 480 B.C. when the Persians invaded Greece and occupied Athens. After defeating and expelling the invaders, for a generation the Athenians left the ruins on

now Turkey), then a Greek region known as Ionia. Ionic columns were lighter and more slender than Doric ones. Also, a typical Ionic column had a decorative base and its capital was not plain but rather featured an elegant spiral or scroll-like shape. Another distinctive aspect of the Ionic style was that

Architectural Tricks Fool the Eye

Over time, Greek architects learned from experience that in large buildings perfectly straight lines often do not look straight to the eye. Depending on the size and shape of a building's features, long horizontal floor or roof lines can appear to sag slightly in the middle. Also, a straight cylindrical column seen against the sky often appears thinner in the middle than at the top and bottom. To counteract these optical illusions, the builders of the Parthenon carefully planned and executed small corrective alterations, called refinements. In some places, they actually exaggerated subtle curvatures and proportions to create illusions of their own, thereby fooling the eye while making the building more beautiful and imposing. Among the most important of the Parthenon's refinements is the slight swelling of the middles of the column shafts, an effect known as entasis. This not only corrected the weakness that would have resulted from using straight lines but also gave the columns a vital, elastic quality. Also, all of the columns in the temple's colonnade leaned inward slightly (each departing from the vertical by 2⅜ inches), giving the building a heightened feeling of soaring perspective. In addition, the floor curved upward in a gentle arc on each of the building's sides, and the panels in the entablature were actually slightly oblong but appeared square when viewed from ground level. These refinements, along with the structure's other proportions, were executed with incredible precision, having an overall margin of error of less than a quarter of an inch.

The Parthenon looms at upper right in this reconstruction of the Athenian Acropolis.

the hill untouched as a memorial; however, in the 440s B.C. Pericles' ambitious building program called for clearing the ruins and constructing a magnificent new temple complex in their place. The result was three new temples dedicated to the city's patron, Athena—the Temple of Athena Nike (Athena "the Victor"), the Erechtheum, and the Parthenon.

The Parthenon, often called the most perfect building ever erected, was a Doric temple, but it was conceived on a grander scale than other Doric structures. Instead of the standard colonnade having six-by-thirteen columns, it featured eight columns on each end and seventeen on each side. Consequently, every facet of the building was bigger than normal. It required some 22,000 tons of marble and was 237 feet long, 110 feet wide, and 65 feet high. Inside the main room—the cella—stood a 38-foot-tall statue of the goddess, designed by Phidias, the greatest sculptor of the ancient world.

Cutting, Dressing, and Lifting the Stones

Most of the marble used in building the Parthenon came from the quarries of Mt. Pentelikon, located a few miles northeast of Athens. A brief examination of the manner in which the stones were quarried, lifted, dressed, and so forth gives an idea of how the Greeks constructed all of their monumental public buildings. First, the blocks of stone had to be separated from the mountainside. To accomplish this task, workmen used mallets and chisels to cut grooves in the

marble. Next, they drove wooden wedges into the grooves and saturated them with water. As the wedges absorbed the water, they expanded, forcing the stone to crack, after which the workers used crowbars and other tools to finish freeing the stones.

Using large wagons pulled by many oxen, other teams of workmen transported the rough-hewn stones to the worksite. There, teams of stonemasons began dressing, or preparing, the blocks so that they would fit into premeasured spaces in the walls. The tools used in this step were various flat chisels, which the masons struck with large wooden mallets. This work had to be done very precisely because, with few exceptions, Greek builders did not use mortar in temples and other large structures. Instead, the stones fit together tightly, after which workers joined one to another with I-shaped iron clamps. With chisels, they carved slots in the top surfaces of two blocks to be joined; then they inserted the clamps and poured melted lead into the spaces that remained. When the next course of stones was placed above, its stones conveniently covered and hid the clamps in the course below.

While this work was progressing, another group of masons dressed the stones for the building's columns. Each of these rounded pieces was called a drum. A tall column, like those in the Parthenon, consisted of a stack of as many as eleven separate drums, topped by a capital decorated in either the Doric or Ionic style. To cut a drum to the desired diameter, a mason placed one of the still rough and somewhat irregular stone disks on top of a circular stone pattern already pre-

The wooden derrick of a mechanical hoist has been placed on the roof of a temple under construction in this artist's conception.

pared on the ground. Using a sharpened metal tool called a "point," which he struck with a mallet, he slowly chipped away pieces of the disk until its diameter matched that of the pattern below it. As in the case of the wall blocks, two column drums were joined by metal fasteners that were later hidden by the drums stacked above them.

Depending on the size and scale of the building, a single ancient Greek column weighed between 60 and 120 tons and stood up to 30 feet (three stories) high. Not surprisingly, then, lifting the upper drums, as well as the blocks for the upper courses of the structure's walls, was a tremendous challenge in an age without

modern machinery. The builders met this challenge by using simple but effective mechanical hoists. The most common type of hoist consisted of a derrick (a wooden framework with ropes and pulleys attached) that the workmen planted firmly on the ground. One rope led away from the derrick and over a wooden scaffolding beam placed directly above the spot where the builders wanted a stone block or drum to rest. After the stone had been attached to the hoist, teams of oxen or men pulled on the rope, which lifted the stone. Once the block had been guided roughly into place, workmen used crowbars and raw muscle power to make an exact fit.

Stoas Used in Town Planning

In this excerpt from his book The Archaeology of Greece, *University of Missouri scholar William R. Biers describes the two-story Stoa of Attalos in Athens's Agora and tells how, in the Hellenistic Age, the Greeks began using stoas in an ordered attempt at town planning.*

The Stoa of Attalos is a fine example of an advanced form of Hellenistic stoa, measuring 381 by 67 feet and utilizing Pentelic marble [from the quarry of Mt. Pentelikon] for façade and columns. . . . The colonnade on each floor was backed by a series of shops. The Doric order was used on the ground floor on the outside, with Ionic columns on the inside. The upper story had piers [vertical supports] with Ionic half-columns on each end and marble balustrades [railings] between them. . . . In the second century B.C. the Athenian Agora took on a more ordered look, with stoas defining the south and east boundaries. This use of the stoa to surround or define a space reflects the contemporary interest in space and planning. Stoas played a great part in the unified complexes that are found where new Hellenistic cities or sanctuaries were laid out. A concern for the relationship of buildings in structural settings together with an interest in visual effects developed in the Hellenistic period.

The Stoa of Attalos, in Athens's Agora, was reconstructed between 1953 and 1956. It houses a museum of artifacts found in the Agora.

Other Public Structures

Of the other public buildings erected by the Greeks, some looked, at least externally, like temples, even though they had little or nothing to do with religion. For example, treasuries were small but ornate structures built to store gold and other riches. These valuables were often offerings that had been made to gods at major religious shrines attended by all Greeks. Treasuries were also designed to show off the wealth, power, and piety of the city-states that erected them. Many states, including Athens, built treasuries at Delphi (in central Greece), home of the famous oracle (a goddess who supposedly could convey the words of Apollo to humans); and at Olympia, where Greeks from far and wide gathered to compete in the prestigious athletic games. Fountain houses also looked like miniature temples and were decorated either in the Doric or Ionic order. These were small structures built beside streams (or aqueducts) that stored water, which people who lived nearby carried away in buckets.

Another important kind of public building came into vogue in the Classical Age—the hall, or interior meeting place. Most halls were council-houses where city magistrates met. But some were used for other purposes, such as public banquets or religious gatherings. Typically such buildings were square in shape, with rows of columns outside and inside (the outside ones being basically decorative and the inside ones both structural and decorative in function). Noted architectural historian A.W. Lawrence describes the council-house (*Boule*) at Athens, erected perhaps in the early fifth century B.C. in the Agora (marketplace):

It was square (78 by 76 ½ feet), with a partition some twenty feet inwards which cut off a lobby along one side. Apparently the speakers stood beside the middle of the partition, while the audience sat on benches parallel with the three outer walls. . . . The eminently practical scheme of this council-house may have set the ultimate pattern for buildings of its class [across Greece].[10]

Another common public building seen in Greek cities, as well as at religious sanctuaries and other places where lots of people gathered, was the stoa, a long, relatively narrow building. Running along its front was a walkway open to the street, town square, or whatever. The walkway had a roof held up by a graceful row of Doric or Ionic columns. To the rear of the walkway were a few or many (depending on the individual building) small chambers. The original purpose of stoas was to provide people with shelter from the sun and rain. But soon they also became meeting places, where informal discussions, educational lectures, and business dealings took place. In the case of the latter, the rear chambers were used as tiny shops and market stalls. A famous stoa built on the north side of the Athenian Agora was called the Stoa Poikile, or "Painted Stoa," because it housed a series of large, impressive paintings.

Some of Greece's larger tombs also utilized monumental stonework and Doric or

The so-called Treasury of Atreus at Mycenae is a well-preserved tholos-style tomb.

Ionic styles of decoration. In the Bronze Age, some Mycenaean kings created large conical- or dome-shaped tombs called *tholoi*. These were underground structures made of large rough-hewn stones set in courses that overlapped one another slightly until they met at the top of the dome. The largest known example is the so-called Treasury of Atreus (misnamed, since it was not a treasury), at Mycenae in southeastern Greece. The main chamber of the *tholos* is 47.5 feet in diameter and 43 feet high and has one stone (above the inner door) weighing a whopping 100 tons. The tombs of the Macedonian kings (the royal line that produced Philip II and Alexander the Great), in northern Greece, are smaller but no less impressive. Dating from Hellenistic times, these generally had four Doric or Ionic columns in front, along with lavish sculptures and or paintings.

The Hellenistic Age also witnessed the development of still another important Greek architectural form—the altar. In earlier eras, these had been relatively small pedestal-like stones set up near the temples. Over time, some were set on wide, low platforms, around which sculptors or painters completed narrow but ornate friezes. The biggest, most ornate versions appeared in the Hellenistic period. Largest and most impressive of all was the Great Altar of Zeus, erected by Eumenes II, ruler of the kingdom of Pergamum (in northwestern Asia Minor). It consisted of a grand staircase topped by an enormous and stately colonnaded podium. Running around the podium was a splendid sculpted frieze showing Zeus and Athena doing battle with an army of giants, a work whose skilled execution and sheer beauty rivaled that of the Parthenon.

Most people today are surprised to learn that large public structures like the Pergamum altar and Parthenon were usually painted in bright colors. The entablatures of temples were most often red and blue with touches of green and gold, for example. The paint eroded away long ago, leaving the pale, often drab naked stone. These splashes of color, combined with the sculptures and other decorations in their original glory, surely gave these buildings a stunning appearance that the surviving ruins cannot begin to convey.

Chapter
2

Sculpture, Painting, and Ceramics

Today, the styles and themes of Classical Greek art, especially sculpture, but also ceramics (pottery), painting, and other forms, remain standards of excellence against which all later styles are measured or compared. As in the cases of other aspects of Greek civilization, the arts were never stagnant. Artistic styles and emphases were markedly different in the Bronze and Archaic Ages from those in the Classical period; and following the latter, the evolution of art continued into the Hellenistic and Roman eras. Thus, the Greek arts developed over many centuries, always building on earlier forms, styles, and ideas.

Yet the Greeks themselves did not fully appreciate the length and complexity of this development. Instead, they assumed that someone in the dim past had created the arts more or less out of nothing. And they had various legends that seemed to support this contention. Among these stories was that of an ancient race called the Telchines, who supposedly invented many of the arts and were the first people to work with bronze and iron. The Telchines were also said to be wizards or magicians of some sort. It is noteworthy that the first-century B.C. Greek geographer Strabo claimed they originally came from Crete.

This seems to correlate with another myth passed along by Strabo's younger contemporary, the Greek historian Diodorus Siculus, who mentioned another Cretan people, called the Eteocretans, as well as a group of local Cretan gods, the

Dactyls. These men and deities, Diodorus said, were

> responsible for the discovery on this island of a great number of important skills which benefit the common life of men . . . and discovered the use of fire and also the nature of bronze and iron . . . and the technique by which they are worked.[11]

Scholars now know that there were some elements of truth in these myths since Crete was indeed the home of the first culturally advanced people to inhabit the Greek sphere—the Minoans. Faint, distorted memories of this culturally advanced and artistically inclined people, along with the Mycenaeans who competed with and eventually supplanted them, apparently survived into later Greek ages. And it is with these Bronze Age Greeks that any account of the Greek arts must begin.

Examples of Bronze Age Greek Art

One artistic form at which both the Minoans and Mycenaeans excelled was painting, especially wall painting. The proof for this has been found in the ruins of the palace-center at Knossos as well as at the site of Akrotiri on the island of Thera (modern Santorini), which lies a few miles north of Knossos. (Akrotiri was a Minoan town that was buried ca. 1600–1500 B.C. by an enormous eruption of the Theran volcano and was rediscovered in the late 1960s.)

Many of the rooms in the Knossos palace were decorated with frescoes (paintings done on wet plaster). These were brightly colored, vibrant, and showed real people and animals moving through natural, informal settings (in contrast to the more idealized and formal Classical style that would develop later). "In Minoan paintings," William Biers points out,

> spontaneity and love of life are expressed. . . . They are naturalistic but the artist was not afraid of changing colors or distorting natural shapes in order to convey feelings or emotions. Many of the

The so-called "Priest-King" fresco was discovered at Knossos by famed archaeologist Sir Arthur Evans.

frescoes exhibit a quick, sketchy technique that forced the artist to concentrate on the particular parts of the picture that were most important to him. . . . Paintings found on Crete vary in size from life-sized figures to miniature frescoes in which the figures are quite small. Floors may also have been painted.[12]

Among the best surviving examples of Minoan wall painting are a series of magnificent frescoes found at Akrotiri and now on display in Athens's National Archaeological Museum. One shows two young boys in a friendly boxing match. Another depicts some women wearing elegant dresses and jewelry and casually gathering flowers. And still another captures a tableau of an island with one or more cities and several ships approaching or departing the shore.

Also impressive was Minoan sculpture, which consisted mostly of small, elegant figurines rather than large-scale statues. These, as well as the local pottery, were made of terra-cotta (baked clay), either unglazed or covered with a glaze made from crushed quartz (a technique known as faience). With the exception of larger jars for storage and pouring, the ceramic items were extremely thin and delicate and painted either with scenes like those in the frescoes or abstract or stylized designs. The themes of these designs included reeds, grasses, and flowers as well as marine plants and animals, especially the octopus.

Minoan artistic styles (along with clothing styles and other cultural aspects) exerted a strong influence on those of the Greek-

This Minoan figurine depicts a snake goddess. Minoan priestesses probably wore similar attire.

speaking Mycenaeans on the mainland. There were some noticeable differences, however. Most significantly, Mycenaean art was often dominated by military and hunting themes. Among other examples, this can be seen in the famous gold Vapheio cups, found in the southern Peloponnesus (the large peninsula making up the southern third

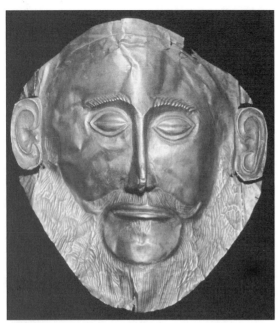

The gold "Mask of Agamemnon" was found at Mycenae by German archaeologist Heinrich Schliemann.

Art in Archaic Times

In the Dark Age that followed the collapse of Greece's Bronze Age civilization, monumental architecture, wall painting, and most other art forms disappeared. Ceramics were still produced, however, and a few examples of vases, cups, storage jars, and so on from the era have survived. From about 1050 to 900 B.C., such objects were often painted, but the techniques and designs were simple and uninspired, consisting mainly of abstract, repetitive arcs, half circles, concentric circles, and the like. In the two centuries that followed (900–700 B.C., which scholars refer to as the Geometric period of Greek art), the designs on pottery featured more geometrical patterns and shapes. Prominent, for instance, were triangles, squares, crosshatching, zigzags, and the familiar pattern known as the Greek key.

In about 800 B.C., coinciding with the beginning of the Archaic Age (and latter part of the Geometric artistic period) in Greece, pottery began to bear likenesses of living things. Among these were deer, horses, birds, and eventually people. And by about 720 B.C., thanks to the Greeks' increasing contacts with Near Eastern peoples, Eastern artistic styles began to influence Greek art. This influence (and artistic period), which scholars call "Orientalizing," included the depiction of common Near Eastern animals and decorative motifs. One popular Eastern motif borrowed was the dot rosette—a central dot encircled by other dots.

The most distinctive pottery style in the later years of the Archaic Age was called "black figure" because figures of people, ani-

of the Greek mainland). By carefully hammering the reverse side of the gold sheets used to produce the cups, the artist created a raised design on the front that shows a stunningly detailed hunting scene in which young men capture wild bulls.

Besides gold goblets, Mycenaean artists produced gold-inlaid swords and solid-gold funerary masks (which were placed over the faces of deceased kings in their tombs). The most famous example is the so-called of mask of Agamemnon (a king mentioned in Homer's famous epic poem about the Trojan War, the *Iliad*), discovered at Mycenae (in the eastern Peloponnesus) in the late 1800s. It seems to have been made by hammering a thin sheet of gold over a wooden carving of a face.

mals, and objects were painted in black onto the natural reddish orange surface of the baked clay. The artist then used a pointed tool to etch details into the figures. This method was pioneered by Athenian artisans, among them Sophilos, who was the first potter known to have signed his work. Black-figure pottery was most popular in the period from 550 to 525 B.C., when an unnamed artisan now called the Amasis Painter was working. A surviving amphora (large storage jar) bears a beautifully rendered scene by the Amasis Painter showing the fertility god Dionysus cavorting with satyrs (creatures half man and half goat).

Large-scale sculpture also developed in Archaic times (paralleling the rise of monumental architecture). The Archaic style was exemplified by stiff and formal yet elegant life-size human figures—the kouroi ("young men") and *korai* ("maidens"). In a typical statue of this kind, Chester Starr explains, "the hands were held stiffly at the sides, the left leg was slightly advanced, the muscles of the chest were merely suggested, and the face and hair were stylized."[13] As time went on, however, these sculptures grew more realistic. An excellent example from late Archaic times is the Anavysos kouros, now in Athens's National Archaeological Museum. It has more detail than earlier kouroi, including the depiction of tear ducts, although the body retains the traditional stiff, unimaginative stance.

Classical Sculpture

Beginning in about 480 B.C., in the opening of the Classical Age, there occurred a major transition in Greek sculpture (as well as in other kinds of art). The static, often stiff, and minimally detailed sculpted figures of the past gave way to more realistic and dynamic-looking ones. In general, carvings of the human figure now began to achieve larger-than-life qualities of beauty, grace, and nobility. Art historian Thomas Craven describes what later came to be called the "Classical ideal":

One of the finest surviving examples of a kouros *statue from the Archaic Age.*

From the mastery of movement and anatomy . . . artists proceeded to ideal forms and faces—to the creation of figures, male and female, beyond those produced by nature . . . to marbles which reveal living flesh within the polished surfaces, faces of god-like serenity, women in costumes of infinite grace. [14]

Classical sculpture included both free-standing statues, some gracing the grounds of religious sanctuaries, such as the ones at Olympia and Delphi, and statues mounted on temples and other monumental structures. The Parthenon's two pediments had many mounted statues, for instance. Each pediment contained about twenty-two major figures and depicted one of the central myths associated with the goddess Athena. Other sculpted figures were carved in bas-relief (raised partly from the flat surfaces of the stones) in friezes on temples and other public buildings. Again, the Parthenon was the outstanding example, with hundreds of exquisite relief figures appearing in two friezes, one on the outside of the entablature, the other on the inside, behind the colonnade.

The first step in creating such sculptures was to make small clay models based on the chief sculptor's design. Once he approved these, he chose the marble blocks out of which the actual statues would be carved. Next, a full-size clay model was created for each sculpted figure (consisting of clay covering an inner frame composed of wood or metal). Carefully copying these models, apprentices chipped away the initial layers of marble from the stone blocks. Eventually, the master sculptor himself took over and applied the final proportions and detail.

In the last step, other craftsmen decorated and accessorized the finished sculptures. In the case of the Parthenon, with its many carved humans and horses, metalworkers attached bronze spears, horse harnesses, and other details to holes the sculptors had drilled in the appropriate places. Then painters applied coatings of wax and bright colors, bringing the statues to life. The polished wax represented flesh, giving the effect of suntanned skin, and hair, lips, and eyebrows were painted a deep red. Clothes on carved human figures were colored varying shades of red, blue, and yellow.

Phidias's Giant Statues

The magnificent, timeless sculptures adorning the exterior of the Parthenon were designed and executed by the great sculptor Phidias. He also designed the colossal statue of Athena that stood inside the building as well as other giant sculptures that his contemporaries and other ancients viewed with nothing less than awe. Unfortunately, the thirty-eight-foot-high statue of Athena that once dominated the interior of the Parthenon did not survive the ages. Luckily, however, a few miniature copies have survived. These, aided by a description of the statue by the second-century A.D. Greek traveler Pausanias, give a fairly good approximation of its appearance. "As you go into the temple," Pausanias writes,

[you can see that] the statue is made of ivory and gold. She [Athena] has a

The Sculptor's Drill

Like other ancient sculptors, Greek ones employed standard tools, including chisels of various shapes and widths. Another extremely useful item was the drill, as explained here by Carl Bluemel in his informative book Greek Sculptors at Work.

It is the simplest of tools . . . nothing more than a sharp, flat chisel, terminating in a short point. It is whirled between the palms of the hands and bores holes in the stone. In order to put more power behind it, the tool is usually given the cranked form of a joiner's drill with a large round knob or grip. The sculptor can then brace it against his chest and revolve it with his hand. Modern sculptors call this tool an auger. If several holes are bored in sections where the work must be carried to some depth in the stone . . . the point can be applied much further in. . . . The long, narrow grooves of folds, especially, can be more easily worked with a drill than with any other tool, because holes may be drilled close together and the small sections of stone remaining between them can then be removed [with another tool].

sphinx on the middle of her helmet, and griffins worked on either side of it. . . . The griffins are wild monsters like lions with wings and the beak of an eagle. . . . The statue of Athena stands upright in an ankle-length tunic with the head of Medusa [a mythical monster] carved in ivory on her breast[plate]. She [Athena] has a [statue of the goddess] Victory about eight feet high [in one hand] and a spear in her [other] hand, and a shield at her feet, and a snake beside the shield. [15]

On the surfaces of the huge shield, Phidias carved (or painted) detailed and dramatic battle scenes. On the outside was a battle between the Athenians and the Amazons, a famous mythical race of warrior women; on the inside was the Gigantomachy, a mythical battle between the gods and a race of giants. (Plutarch later reported that two of the figures fighting the Amazons looked exactly like Phidias and his friend, the politician Pericles.)

To build a statue of such immense size required the initial creation of a full-size clay replica. This job alone probably took Phidias and his bevy of assistants up to two years to complete. These helpers then made negative plaster molds of various sections of the model and used them to produce the pieces for the finished statue. For example, they placed sheets of gold into the molds of

This scale model shows Phidias's Athena statue towering over him.

the one of Zeus that sat on a huge throne in the Temple of Zeus at Olympia, a work later named one of the seven wonders of the ancient world. Like the giant Athena, the monumental Zeus has not survived. But fortunately, Strabo penned this description:

> The greatest [of the offerings in the temple of Zeus at Olympia] was the image of Zeus, which Phidias . . . made of ivory, and which is of such great size that, though the temple is indeed one of the largest, the artist seems to have failed to take into account the question of proportion; for although he represented the god as seated, he [Zeus] almost touches the peak of the roof, and thus gives the impression that, if he were to stand up straight, he would take the roof off the temple. . . . Panainos the painter, Phidias's own brother and his coworker, was a great help to him in the decoration of the statue, especially the drapery [of the god's tunic], with colors. [16]

Classical Painting

Panainos not only worked on the giant Zeus but also adorned the site of Olympia with a number of huge paintings that became famous across the Greek world. One showed the mythical character Atlas holding up the heavens, with the great hero Heracles (the Roman Hercules) about to relieve him of the burden. Pausanias also mentioned a painting showing Heracles slaying the fearsome Nemean lion (one of the hero's famous twelve labors).

the goddess's dress and used small hammers to beat the soft metal until it conformed to the mold's outlines. In all, some twenty-five hundred pounds of gold were needed. When all the pieces were ready, craftsmen used metal clamps and wooden dowels to assemble them on a huge wooden framework carved to duplicate the clay model's size and proportions.

The same techniques were employed to produce another of Phidias's giant statues—

The Parthenon Frieze

This description of the figures on the Parthenon's Ionic frieze (located on the upper inside portion of the temple's outer colonnade) is by scholar Ian Jenkins of the British Museum, from his book about the frieze.

The two branches of the frieze present a procession [parade] composed of various groups of figures arranged in a sequence. On the [building's] west side we see horsemen, some paired, others shown singly. The directional flow is from right to left, or south to north. . . . The long north side carries forward the cavalcade begun on the west, and the horsemen occupy nearly half of the total number of slabs. Ahead of them come chariots, then groups of figures walking in procession, including elders, musicians, pitcher-bearers, tray-bearers and figures leading cattle and sheep as sacrificial victims. Turning the corner onto the east side we find . . . a procession of girls carrying vessels . . . [and] male figures leaning on staves [walking sticks] and engaged in conversation. . . . Ahead of them are shown the gods, whose seated pose allows them to appear larger than the mortal figures in the frieze. . . . The southern branch of the frieze follows a pattern similar to that of the north. The two processions do not actually meet, since the gods are placed between them.

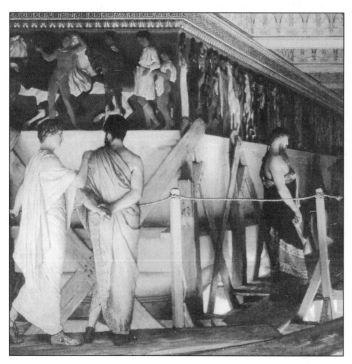

Sir Lawrence Alma-Tadema's nineteenth-century painting of Phidias showing fellow Athenians the Parthenon frieze.

Perhaps the most famous and gifted of all the Classical Greek painters was Polygnotus, who was a contemporary of Panainos, Phidias, and Pericles. One of the innovations attributed to Polygnotus was the technique of spreading his figures across the painting rather than placing them all in a single horizontal line as earlier painters had. In the words of University of Louisville scholar Robert B. Kebric:

A nineteenth-century engraving of Phidias's giant statue of Zeus at Olympia.

Besides freeing the figures in his paintings from the archaic stiffness of the past, Polygnotus . . . [arranged] individuals, or groups of individuals, on different levels, scattering them about at various points in space. . . . Landscape figures such as trees and rocks gave an additional feeling of depth. Also, an emotional quality appears to have characterized his work, with figures reacting to what has just happened or what is about to happen. . . . His work became so valued that it was frequently restored, and even during the early Roman Empire, the eminent [orator] Quintilian advised that any serious study of painting must begin with Polygnotus.[17]

Polygnotus's most famous painting was the *Capture of Troy,* on display at Delphi. Like his other murals, along with those of Panainos and other Classical painters, the work was lost long ago, leaving behind only a few literary descriptions. The most detailed is by Pausanias:

The painting . . . shows the fall of Troy and the Greeks sailing away. Menelaus's men are getting ready for the voyage [back to Greece; Menelaus was the king of Sparta and husband of Helen, whose abduction by a Trojan prince ignited the siege of Troy]. There is a painting of the ship with a mixture of men and boys among the sailors, and the ship's steersman Phrontis standing amidships holding two poles. . . . [Some men] are

Women Painters

Very few of the artists and artisans in ancient Greece were women. There were exceptions, however, as revealed by the Roman scholar Pliny the Elder in this excerpt from his Natural History *(translated by Maureen B. Fant in her* Women's Life in Greece and Rome*).*

Women, too, have been painters. Timarete, the daughter of [the famous painter] Micon, painted a [likeness of the goddess] Diana on a panel . . . in Ephesus. Irene, daughter and student of [the dramatist] Cratinus, painted a girl at Eleusis. . . . Iaia of Cyzicus, who never married, worked in Rome [in the early first century B.C.]. She used both the painter's brush and, on ivory, the graving tool. She painted women most frequently, including a panel picture of an old woman in Naples, and even a self-portrait for which she used a mirror. No one's hand was quicker to paint a picture than hers; so great was her talent that her prices far exceeded those of the most celebrated [male] painters of her day.

taking down Menelaus's tent not far from the ship. . . . [The maiden] Briseis is standing with Diomedes above her and Iphis in front of them as if they are all gazing at Helen's beauty. Helen herself is standing with Eurybates near her. . . . Above Helen sits a man wrapped in a purple cloak, extremely melancholy; you would know it was [Trojan king] Priam's son Helenos even before you read the inscription. [18]

Hellenistic Art: The Culmination of Realism

Over the course of many centuries, the evolution of Greek sculpture and painting had witnessed a constant development toward increased realism. This trend continued throughout the Classical period and reached its culmination in the subsequent Hellenistic Age. In prior eras sculptors and painters had almost always chosen divine or heroic subjects, which were portrayed in ideal situations and poses. In Hellenistic times, by contrast, there was an increased emphasis in Greek society on the individual person and his or her needs and happiness; and this was reflected to some degree in art. "For the first time," says Biers,

all classes of society and all gradations of physical condition were realistically shown, and often caricatured. . . . Observation of everyday life and interest in various types of people are evident. . . . A sculpture of a boy playing

The remains of the great altar from Pergamum were sent to Berlin, Germany, in 1902, where they rest in a museum specially built for them.

with a goose shows the typical plump child of the period. . . . At the other end of the scale is the Drunken Old Woman. . . . [She] sits on the ground cradling a wreathed wine bottle as if it were a child. The extreme ageing of the face and neck and the position of the head, thrown back in a drunken stupor, make a powerful impression on the viewer.[19]

Despite many such realistic depictions of ordinary people, the Classical approach of showing well-proportioned gods and heroes was still very much alive in Hellenistic times; the artists simply took that approach to more realistic and sometimes more emotional and dramatic extremes. The new style reached its height in the great sculpted frieze winding around the base of the famous altar at Pergamum. This incredible depiction of the Gigantomachy contains seventy-five figures in all, each an artistic masterpiece. In addition to the multitude of details, one is struck by the dynamism of the figures. They seem to flow and writhe, giving the impression that at any moment they might detach themselves from the stone and walk away. (Indeed, at various points the artists made arms or legs reach out and touch part of the altar's steps.) Also extraordinary is the range of emotions shown, with some faces registering clearcut anger, fear, or agony. "Technically, Greek art had never reached such heights," Biers points out. "It was this art that had such influence on the Romans, and through them on the Italian Renaissance."[20]

Various pieces of evidence suggest that Greek paintings also became more realistic and dramatic in the Hellenistic Age. Almost all of these works have been lost. But a few, or at least portions of them, have survived indirectly in the form of later Roman copies, often in floor or wall mosaics. For example, some clues suggest that a late fourth-century B.C. (early Hellenistic) master, Philoxenos of Eretria, executed a huge painting of Alexander the Great defeating the Persian king Darius III. The painting itself is long since gone. But modern archaeologists found a large floor mosaic in the ruins of Pompeii. Made up of about 1.5 million individual tiny pieces of colored stone and glass, it seems to be a copy of Philoxenos's lost work. If so, it proves that ancient Greek painters reached a level of proficiency and realism that to modern eyes rivals that of Europe's Renaissance masters.

Classical Ceramics

A smaller-scale and more refined style of painting was an essential facet of Greek ceramics, beginning at least with the Geometric and black-figure work of the Archaic Age. In the Classical Age, new styles emerged as the demand for ceramic vessels of all kinds increased. (These included vases for holding flowers and fruit, drinking cups, dinner plates, cooking pots, sauce pans, storage jars, containers for religious offerings and other sacred vessels, bowls for mixing wine, and many others.)

One important new pottery style was the "red figure," essentially a reversal of the black-figure approach. A red-figure pot left the figures of humans and animals in the fired pot's natural reddish tone and rendered the backgrounds black. This allowed for the application of more realistic details, which were applied with a brush (although etching was still employed for certain fine details). Red-figure pottery was perfected in the early 400s B.C. by various Athenian artisans. One, whom modern scholars call the Berlin Painter, excelled at painting human limbs and muscles. Another artisan of the period, the so-called Brygos Painter, specialized in creating detailed scenes on the bottoms of drinking cups.

A red-figure vase dated to circa 335 B.C. shows a scene from an ancient Greek play.

Greek Pottery Kiln

Still another pottery style that gained popularity in the Classical Age was the "white-ground" technique. It featured figures painted in delicate dark lines against a white background. White-ground paintings were most often used on the special ceramic containers that mourners placed in tombs.

Whatever the style of the painting applied to ceramic containers, the potters of Classical and Hellenistic times made these pots in the same basic manner as their predecessors. They began with wet clay (*ceramos*), which they worked on a potter's wheel. This was "a flat wheel revolving on a vertical spindle," scholar Robert Flaceliere explains, "which the potter either turned by hand himself or employed an assistant to operate for him. When a pot had been modeled, it was set in the sun to dry." [21] After it was dry, most potters placed the pot in a wood-burning kiln, which reached a temperature of perhaps one thousand degrees Fahrenheit. This produced a durable, long-lasting product, examples of which still exist in museums around the world. Some are so well preserved they look as if they were made only yesterday, which never fails to surprise and impress modern visitors. In this way, through the immortality of their creations, artists long dead continue to speak to each new generation.

Chapter

3

Literature and the Pursuit of Knowledge

If the architectural and artistic heritage the ancient Greeks left the Western world can be described as major and inspiring, their literary and intellectual legacy is nothing less than tremendous. The Greeks created the first examples of Western literature. They then proceeded to establish nearly all of the literary forms and disciplines adopted in later Western cultures, including today's. Poetry, philosophy, scientific inquiry, historical writing, tragic and comedic drama, oratorical prose (speech writing), literary criticism, and prose fiction, including the novel—all were invented and brought to early perfection by the Greeks. Most of the manuscripts from these genres perished in the wake of Rome's fall and the disintegration of the ancient world.

But some of the major ones survived. And Europeans began to rediscover these remnants during the fourteenth century, providing models for the rebirth of learning and high culture that today is known as the Renaissance.

Early Versions of Written Greek

It goes without saying that the Greeks could not have produced so much rich and varied literature and ideas without two essential tools—the Greek language itself and a practical alphabet to transform its words into written form. The precursors of the Greek language originated somewhere in western Asia in a group of related tongues that scholars label Indo-European. The Mycenaeans

These characters written in Linear B were discovered at Pylos, in southern Greece.

brought with them or developed an early version of Greek when they settled the Greek mainland in the early second millennium B.C. And sometime in the mid part of that millennium, they created a script that modern scholars dubbed Linear B. Unfortunately, though it constituted the earliest form of written Greek, it was very complex and not designed to produce literature. Scholars Lesley and Roy A. Adkins explain:

> Over 90 signs were used, written left to right . . . and the script was used for official accounts and inventories. It seems that writing was not widespread, but

done mainly by bureaucratic officials associated with palaces; it was not used for, or suitable for, literary purposes. Virtually all of the inscriptions relate to administration (lists of people, produce, and manufactured goods). [22]

After the fall of Greece's Bronze Age civilization, whatever literacy that existed was lost, and for some three centuries no writings of any kind were produced. Then, perhaps in about 800 B.C., at the start of the Archaic Age, the Greeks reinvented writing. This time they employed a simpler, more practical alphabet that they borrowed from the Phoenicians, an industrious Near Eastern maritime people. (The Greek word for "letters" was *phoinikia,* literally meaning "Phoenician things.")

The new alphabet made it possible to express the still developing Greek language in written form. Several dialects existed across the Greek sphere, but the differences were small enough that Greeks everywhere could understand one another. Eventually, in the early Hellenistic Age, most of the old dialects declined in favor of a more standard, universal version, called koine, based on the Attic dialect (the one spoken in Athens). Whatever version was used, Greek showed itself to have both the flexibility and lyrical qualities perfectly suited to creating literature. It is "clear, supple, and musical," Robert Flaceliere points out.

It took shape for literary purposes in the service of poetry, yet was able to adapt itself effortlessly to the eloquence

Achilles Slays Hector

The scene in which the Greek warrior Achilles fights and kills the Trojan prince Hector is one of the highlights of Homer's Iliad. *This excerpt from their epic confrontation (taken from Robert Fagles's acclaimed translation), gives some idea of the great poet's descriptive and dramatic powers.*

So Hector swooped now, swinging his whetted sword, and Achilles charged too, bursting with rage, barbaric, guarding his chest with the well-wrought blazoned shield. . . . Bright as that . . . brightest star that rides the heavens, so fire flared up from the sharp point of the spear Achilles brandished high in his right hand, bent on Hector's death, scanning his splendid body—where to pierce it best? . . . One spot lay exposed . . . the open throat, where the end of life comes quickest—*there,* as Hector charged in fury, brilliant Achilles drove his spear and the point went stabbing clean through the tender neck; but the heavy bronze weapon failed to slash the windpipe—Hector could still gasp out some words, some last reply. . . . At the point of death, Hector, his helmet flashing, said, "I know you well—I see my fate before me. . . . But now beware, or my curse will draw god's wrath upon your head, that day when Paris and lord Apollo—for all your fighting heart—destroy you at the

Scaean Gates!" Death cut him short. The end closed in around him. Flying free of his limbs, his soul went wringing down to the House of Death.

The Greek champion Achilles (on chariot) attacks the Trojan warrior Hector in this nineteenth-century Italian painting.

of [the great orator] Demosthenes or the philosophical thought of Plato. [It is] a tongue fluid as a spring, melodious as a song, yet . . . as strictly organized as a temple built of highly polished and precisely laid blocks of stone.[23]

Homer's Works and Other Early Epics

By the phrase "in the service of poetry," Flaceliere refers to Homer's famous epic poems, the *Iliad* and the *Odyssey*. The *Iliad* tells the story of how, in the last year of the war between the Greeks and the Trojans, the proud Greek warrior Achilles quarreled with the leader of the expedition and refused to fight. Only after his friend Patroclus was slain did Achilles change his mind, reenter the fray, and avenge Patroclus's death by killing the Trojan champion Hector. The *Odyssey* begins after Troy's fall and traces the ten-year-long adventures of another leader of the Greek expedition, Odysseus.

The first examples of Western literature, these works appeared sometime in the eighth century B.C. At first, they were transmitted in oral form by traveling bards, who recited them for eager audiences. Eventually, perhaps in the sixth century B.C., someone wrote them down. The two epics are long, majestic, highly evolved literary masterpieces, critically acclaimed by the ancient and modern worlds alike as supremely brilliant in both conception and execution. Considering this, it is hardly surprising that they had a profound effect on Greek (as well as Roman) culture throughout antiquity. People saw them as vital sources of literary, artistic, moral, social, educational, and political instruction as well as practical wisdom. Indeed, Homer's influence and reputation in the ancient world became so great that he overshadowed all other writers and people came to refer to him simply and reverently as "the Poet."

Though unarguably the greatest, Homer was not the only popular epic poet. The early years of Greek literature produced many others, most of whose works have not survived. (Historians know about them because they are mentioned and quoted in the works of other ancient writers.) Some of these works belonged to the so-called Epic Cycle, which described mythological events from the beginning of the world until the close of the Age of Heroes (the name the Greeks gave to the late Bronze Age). Six of the epics dealt with those events surrounding the Trojan War and its aftermath that Homer had not covered: the *Cypria, Aethiopis, Sack of Troy, Little Iliad, Nostoi,* and *Telegony.* The other poems of the Epic Cycle, which are also lost, covered the ages of gods and heroes preceding the Trojan War. The *Titanomachy* told about the emergence of the Titans, an early race of gods, and their war with the Olympian gods led by Zeus. The other three epics in the cycle—the *Oedipodea* (*Story of Oedipus*), *Thebaïs,* and *Epigoni*—formed the nucleus of the Theban Myth Cycle, centered on the early rulers of the major city of Thebes. Scholars believe that the later Athenian playwright Sophocles drew much of the material for his three Theban plays (*Oedipus the King, Oedipus at Colonus,* and *Antigone*) from these epics.

Sir Lawrence Alma-Tadema's nineteenth-century painting of a private recitation of Homer's epic poetry in ancient Greece.

Luckily, the works of one early minor epic poet have survived. Hesiod was born near Thebes in the late eighth century B.C., perhaps when Homer was an old man (although this is by no means certain). The Greeks held that a person's talent at singing, acting, writing poetry, or other artistic endeavors was a gift endowed by Zeus's daughters, the Muses. And Hesiod, a conservative, hard working farmer, believed that these deities had given him the gift of "sweet song" one day while he was tending his sheep. This inspired him to write the *Theogony,* which tells about the creation of the world and early exploits of the gods. Hesiod also wrote the *Works and Days;* the main theme is the virtue of hard work, which the author illustrates by describing the proper way to run a farm.

Lyric Poetry

Even as the epic poets were spinning their long tales of gods, heroes, war, and great adventure, other poets were beginning to produce much shorter verses or songs, mostly about personal emotions and experiences and themes from everyday life. Because these were originally meant to be recited or sung to the accompaniment of the lyre—a small harp—the genre became known as lyric poetry. Several different forms of lyric verses developed featuring various meters (distinctive rhythms).

One type, the elegy, became a potent medium for expressing personal feelings, the glories of war, tomb epitaphs, laments, and love songs. Among the more popular of the early lyric poets was Archilochus, who flourished during the 600s B.C. In the following example of his work, he treats a serious subject with witty humor as he presents a soldier's (perhaps his own?) rationale for tossing away his weapons while retreating from battle: "Well, what if some barbaric Thracian glories in the perfect shield I left under a bush? I was sorry to leave it—but I saved my skin. Does it matter? O hell, I'll buy a better one!"[24] Much later, in the Hellenistic period, the love elegy became widely popular. This earthy example is by the first-century B.C. poet Meleager: "The wine cup is happy. It rubbed against warm Zenophila's erotic mouth. O bliss! I wish she would press her lips under my lips and in one breathless gulp drain down my soul."[25]

Another common form of lyric poetry was the choral ode, originally composed to be sung and danced to at religious festivals by choirs of men, boys, or girls. As time went on, the term referred to any lyrics sung by a group of people and accompanied by musical instruments. Among the many kinds of choral ode were paeans (hymns of praise), dirges (sad songs sung at funerals), wedding songs, and victory odes (*epinikia*). The fifth-century B.C. Theban poet Pindar gained a reputation as the master of the victory ode. He wrote a great many to honor winning athletes at Olympia and other major sporting venues. The following example, the *Sixth Nemean Ode*, celebrates the victory of a young wrestler named Alkimidas:

> Single is the race, single of men and gods; from a single mother we both draw breath. But a difference of power in everything keeps us apart. . . . Yet we can in greatness of mind or of body be like the Immortals, though we know not to what goal . . . fate has written that we shall run. Even now, Alkimidas gives visible witness that his race is like the fruitful fields. . . . He has come from Nemea's well-loved games, a boy in struggle. . . . He has been revealed a hunter and had good sport in wrestling.[26]

The early Greek thinker Thales proposed that water was nature's underlying principle.

The First Philosopher-Scientists

In addition to poetry, the Greeks produced huge amounts of prose covering a wide range of subjects. Among the earliest of these writings were those expressing new philosophic and scientific ideas that spread rapidly through the Greek world in late Archaic and early Classical times. At first, the Greeks made no clear distinction between philosophy and science. Like modern scientists, early Greek thinkers made observations about the natural world; and like modern philosophers, they speculated on the workings of the world and meaning of life without producing verifiable evidence to support their proposals.

More important was the then-novel approach to knowledge these thinkers used. Earlier peoples, including the Egyptians and Babylonians, had collected many scientific observations over the centuries. But "scientists" in these cultures had automatically attributed natural phenomena, as well as control over human destiny, to various gods, spirits, and other supernatural elements. In contrast, the Greeks largely removed the gods and the supernatural from scientific study and discussion. As modern scientists do, they tended to see the heavenly bodies and other facets of nature as material objects obeying natural laws rather than as personalized beings.

Viewing the universe as a "cosmos," an orderly system governed by natural laws, several generations of Greek truth seekers inquired into diverse aspects of nature. This laid the groundwork for the disciplines of astronomy, physics, chemistry, biology, and medicine. The first major Greek philosopher-scientist, Thales of Miletus (who flourished in about 600 B.C.), concluded that nature's underlying physical principle—the *physis*—was water (in other words, that all matter was based on water in one way or another). Later Greek thinkers disagreed and proposed numerous other substances for the *physis*. Among them were Anaximander (sixth century B.C.), Pythagoras (sixth century B.C.), Anaxagoras (fifth century B.C.), and Democritus (fifth-to-fourth century B.C.). Democritus developed an early version of the atomic theory, suggesting that all matter is composed of tiny, invisible particles called atoms.

Today, these early thinkers are called pre-Socractic because they predated the Athenian philosopher Socrates (fifth century B.C.). His life and teachings marked a crucial watershed in which Greek philosophy and science began to become separate disciplines. This was because Socrates lacked interest in studying nature. He advocated instead that it was more important for people to understand the meaning of ethical concepts like goodness, wisdom, and justice and to find ways to apply these concepts to society. Socrates left no writings of his own. But two of his devoted

The great Athenian philosopher Plato, depicted here, was a follower of Socrates.

followers, Plato and Xenophon (both fourth century B.C.), recorded most of his major ideas in their own works, which were voluminous.

Like Socrates, Plato and his brilliant student, Aristotle, were concerned with moral principles and the human condition. In his dialogue *Meno*, for example, Plato explores whether virtue might be taught in a systematic way. He and Aristotle did not confine themselves strictly to ethics, however. Each generated a huge body of writings covering a wide range of subjects, ranging from politics to literary criticism. And each conducted scientific researches or speculation that exerted a profound influence on later Greek, Roman, and medieval European thinkers.

Aristotle, in a drawing based on a bust, studied under Plato at the latter's school.

Plato's *Timaeus,* for instance, deals with the formation of the universe; and Aristotle made major contributions to the fields of biology and zoology, including a workable system for classifying animals.

The fifth and fourth centuries B.C., encompassing the Classical Age, witnessed other major developments in science-related research and writing. Aristotle's colleague and friend, Theophrastus, produced numerous writings about plants based on personal observations, thereby founding the science of botany. Meanwhile, Greek physicians and medical researchers made important progress of their own by establishing the world's first medical schools. The two most famous were at Cnidus and Cos (both near the Ionian island of Rhodes). Hippocrates, today recognized as the "father" of medicine, oversaw the Cos school during the second half of the fifth century B.C. He and his students produced hundreds of writings on such topics as anatomy, surgery, treatment by diet and drugs, diseases of women and children, and medical ethics.

History and Oratory

The Classical Age produced many other important intellectual-literary accomplishments, including historical works. First came the work of Herodotus (fifth century B.C.). Modern scholars dubbed him the "father" of history because his groundbreaking *Histories* remains the world's oldest surviving conventional historical work. It contains a fairly detailed account of the Greco-Persian Wars of the early fifth century B.C., based partly on the secondhand

A surviving bust of the original and highly influential Athenian thinker Socrates.

testimony of some of the participants. The book also features numerous digressions describing the places the author visited in his wide-ranging travels, including Egypt and other parts of the Near East.

The Athenians Thucydides and Xenophon also played roles in the establishment of the history-writing genre. When the disastrous Peloponnesian War (in which Greeks fought other Greeks) erupted in 431 B.C., Thucydides recognized its historical importance and got to work. He was determined, as Charles Freeman puts it, "to write a documentary history of events as they unfolded," something no one had ever done before.

Whereas Herodotus had included some rumors, legends, and thirdhand information in his own work, Thucydides endeavored to present only those events that he or someone he interviewed had witnessed firsthand. Added to this sound approach was Thucydides' considerable talents as a writer. "In his penetration into the core of human motivation," Freeman continues, "his steady gaze on the horrors of war, and his superb narrative power, Thucydides ranks as one of Europe's major historians."[27] Though not as skilled a historian as Thucydides, Xenophon dutifully chronicled the main events of the great war's final years as well as several pivotal wars and battles of the fourth century B.C.

Two other literary forms gained prominence in the Classical Age, both of which involved speech writing. On the one hand, professionals known as *logographai* prepared long court speeches for ordinary people to deliver when either defending themselves or prosecuting others. A number of these speeches have survived. And some, particularly those by the Athenians Antiphon (fifth century B.C.) and Lysias (fifth-to-fourth century B.C.), are masterpieces of eloquence and persuasion. An excellent example consists of the opening remarks to a jury that Lysias composed in 403 B.C. for a murder case he prosecuted himself:

> I feel no difficulty, members of the jury, in beginning my accusation. The difficulty will be in bringing my speech to an end. Such is the enormity, and so great the number of my opponent's

The Speeches of Demosthenes

In the mid–fourth century B.C., *the Macedonian king Philip II, father of Alexander the Great, threatened to overrun the major city-states of southern Greece. In response, the fiery Athenian orator Demosthenes delivered a series of dramatic speeches in an attempt to rally the Greeks against Philip, whom he portrayed as a barbarian. Among these speeches were the second and third* Olynthiacs, *briefly excerpted here (from J.H. Vince's translation).*

In a word, he [Philip] has hoodwinked everyone who has had any dealings with him. He has played upon the folly of each party in turn and exploited their ignorance of his own character. That is how he has gained his power. . . . What better time or occasion could you find than the present, men of Athens? When will you do your duty, if not now? Has not your enemy already captured all our strongholds, and if he becomes master of the Chalcidice, shall we not be overwhelmed with dishonor? . . . Is not Philip our enemy? And in possession of our property? And a barbarian? Is any description too bad for him? But, in the name of the gods, when we have abandoned all these places and almost helped Philip to gain them, shall we then ask who is to blame?

crimes, that it would be impossible, even if one lied, to make the accusations worse than the facts, and although one wishes to speak the truth, one cannot tell all. Either the accuser must tire or the time must fail. [28]

Another gifted Athenian *logographos,* Demosthenes (fourth century B.C.), was also the foremost Greek practitioner of political oratory. He is most famous for composing and delivering a series of dramatic public speeches (the *Philippics* and *Olynthiacs*) denouncing the conquests of Macedonia's King Philip II.

Hellenistic Science and Literature

Many of the intellectual and literary endeavors of the Archaic and Classical eras continued and even expanded in scope in Hellenistic times. Hellenistic scientists produced many important new ideas and writings, for instance. The main focus of research shifted from mainland Greece to Alexandria, Egypt (then ruled by a Greek dynasty), which rapidly established itself as the cultural and intellectual center of the Mediterranean world. There, Herophilus of Calchedon (third century B.C.), established the Alexandrian medical school. He and his talented pupil, Erasistratus, made major strides in anatomy and physiology. Other important Alexandrian researchers included Euclid (third century B.C.), whose *Elements* remains the most important book on geometry ever written; Eratosthenes (third century B.C.), who measured Earth's circumference with amazing accuracy; and Hipparchus (second century B.C.), who compiled a massive star catalog and invented latitude and longitude.

The foundations for the science of mechanics were also laid by Greek researchers during this period. Ctesibius (third century B.C.) devised the first version of the cylinder and plunger, the basis for numerous machines both ancient and modern (including the cylinders and pistons in internal-combustion engines). This new invention soon began to see use in pumps for irrigation and raising water out of flooded mines. Ctesibius's contemporary, the brilliant mathematician and inventor Archimedes, discovered the basic principles of floating bodies as well as the formulas for the volumes of spheres, cylinders, and other solid figures. Archimedes also experimented with new ways to use levers, pulleys, and other simple machines.

In addition, Archimedes did future ages a service by recording the ideas of an earlier Greek astronomer, Aristarchus, most of whose own writings did not survive. Aristarchus had correctly proposed that the Sun, not Earth, lay at the center of the cosmos, a concept that turned out to be many centuries ahead of its time. In his *Sand-Reckoner*, Archimedes states:

Aristarchus of Samos brought out a book . . . in which the premises led to the result that the universe is many times greater than that now so called. His hypotheses are that the fixed stars and the sun remain unmoved, [and] that the Earth revolves about the sun . . . the sun lying in the middle of the orbit.[29]

The Greek astronomer Hipparchus is credited with inventing longitude and latitude.

Hellenistic literature also took the form of popular poetry and prose. On the one hand, Apollonius of Rhodes (third century B.C.) revived the genre of epic poetry with his *Argonautica,* about the mythical hero Jason and his quest for the fabulous Golden Fleece. On the other, thousands of shorter poems were produced by writers such as Meleager, Callimachus, and Theocritus. At the same time, another writer, Zenodotus, restored, collated, and published new editions of earlier classics, including Homer's epics.

Greek Literature in Roman Times

Most of these scientific and literary works were aimed at a small number of well-educated, highbrow readers. Nevertheless, educational opportunities expanded in the Hellenistic Age, which helped to stimulate the development, for the first time in history, of a fairly sizable general reading public. To meet the increasing demand for materials for readers of limited or average educational achievement, second-rate writers multiplied and became successful. And thereafter, espe-

The mythical shepherd Daphnis and his lover Chloe were frequent subjects of Greek literature.

cially in Greece's Roman period, Greek literature consisted of both high-quality works that appealed to a limited audience and popular pulp for the masses.

Perhaps the most striking example of the new literature aimed at the mass market was an early form of a genre taken for granted today—the novel. Greek novels, which modern scholars usually label "romances," were fictional narratives that almost always dealt with two people in love. Invariably, the lovers found themselves separated in various mishaps and adventures but were fortunately reunited in the end. Most entries in the genre, much like their modern counterparts, tended to be entertaining but forgettable. However, a few were of higher quality, a notable example being *Daphnis and Chloe* by Longus (third century A.D.). This excerpt sets the pleasant pastoral scene in which the title characters fall in love:

It was the beginning of spring and all the flowers were in bloom, in the woods, in the meadows, and on the mountains. Already there was a buzzing of bees . . . a sound of singing-birds . . . filling the thickets with enchanting song. So now that all things were possessed by the beauty of the season, these two tender young creatures [the lovers] began to imitate the sights and sounds around them. Hearing the birds singing, they burst into song . . . and taking their cue from the bees, they started gathering flowers, some of which they dropped into their bosoms, and the rest they wove into garlands. [30]

The Roman period also saw older forms of Greek literature continue to flourish. In the realm of philosophy, Plotinus (third century A.D.) advocated the existence of a mystical, ascending ladder of realities. The highest rung on the ladder was a state of "goodness" resembling that described by Plato centuries before; so Plotinus's belief system came to be known as Neoplatonism. In the sciences, Galen of Pergamum (second century A.D.) conducted much important medical research and composed numerous well-written treatises covering every area of medical inquiry. Meanwhile, the astronomer-geographer Ptolemy (second century A.D.), who lived and worked in Alexandria, published his *Mathematike Syntaxis* (in later ages called the *Almagest*), among other writings. A comprehensive description of the heavenly bodies revolving around Earth, the work's mistaken ideas continued to be accepted as scientific truth until the fifteenth century.

Galen and Ptolemy were not the only prolific and influential Greek writers of the Roman era. Two other outstanding examples were Lucian of Samosata (second century A.D.) and Plutarch of Chaeronea (first century A.D.). Lucian turned out many speeches, letters, essays, stories, and dialogues, most of them satiric, humorous, clever, and entertaining. His *True History* (which is anything but true!), for example, describes voyages to the moon and the Underworld.

In contrast, Plutarch was a biographer and moralist with a serious, thoughtful, and engaging writing style. His large corpus of surviving works includes the *Parallel Lives*,

---

Plutarch Remembers a Great Greek Leader

Plutarch wrote so many thousands of memorable passages in his numerous surviving works that no single example stands out above the others. One memorable one that is rarely quoted is the scene from his biography of Pericles (translated by Ian Scott-Kilvert in The Rise and Fall of Athens*), in which that famous Athenian leader shows quick thinking in quelling a sudden panic among his troops while en route to attack the Spartans.*

Pericles manned 150 warships, embarked a large number of his best hoplites [infantrymen] and horsemen, and was all ready to put to sea. . . . But at the very moment when the ships were fully manned and Pericles had gone on board his own trireme [oared warship], an eclipse of the sun took place, darkness descended, and everyone was seized with panic, since they regarded this as a tremendous portent [bad omen]. When Pericles saw that his helmsman was frightened and quite at a loss at what to do, he held up his cloak in front of the man's eyes and asked him whether he found this alarming or thought it a terrible omen. When he replied that he did not, Pericles asked, "What is the difference, then, between this and the eclipse, except that the eclipse has been caused by something bigger than my cloak?" This is the story, at any rate, which is told in the schools.

---

a series of some fifty biographies of famous Greek and Roman figures. These are not straightforward histories. Yet because Plutarch had access to many ancient sources that are now lost, modern historians are forever in his debt for his preservation of historical information about the ages preceding his own. In intent, method, style, and execution, the works of Plutarch, Lucian, Galen, and other Greeks of their era were the sophisticated end result of nearly a thousand years of Greek intellectual and literary experimentation and output.

Chapter

4

Theater and Drama

Along with epic and lyric poetry, philosophical and scientific treatises, history, oratory, and so forth, the Greeks invented another literary form that continues to engage and entertain people today, namely drama. They also created a whole new expressive art form with which to transform their written plays into performances that people could watch and enjoy—theater. By the advent of Hellenistic times, theaters, playwrights, and actors existed across the Greek-speaking world. Yet they originated and enjoyed their greatest ancient flowering in the city-state of Athens during an astonishingly brief period, from about 530 to 400 B.C. In these years, especially during Athens's cultural golden age, a handful of gifted individuals fashioned the model for great drama and theater for all times.

Early Sources of Drama

The exact manner in which drama and theater emerged in Athens is uncertain. But modern scholars have pieced together a likely scenario that begins in the eighth century B.C. By that time, Greeks everywhere had developed elaborate rituals surrounding the worship of Dionysus, the god of fertility, the vine, and wine. Among these rituals was the recitation of verses known as dithyramb, which the worshippers sang and danced to. Evidently, the words of these sacred songs told the story of Dionysus's life and adventures, which were part of the heritage of

This depiction of the fertility god Dionysus (second from left) and some of his followers comes from a Greek vase. His story was a major source of drama.

myths the Greeks had inherited from earlier ages.

Over time, the dithyrambs became larger in scale by including the stories of other gods as well as a few widely respected human heroes. They also became more stately and dramatic. A priest and a selected group of worshippers stood in front of the rest of the congregation and, to the accompaniment of flutes, cymbals, and other instruments, enacted a god's or hero's story through song and dance. In a sense, therefore, the priest and his assistants were the first performers and the rest of the congregation their audience. A particularly crucial development occurred when the priests began slightly altering, building on, and otherwise enhancing the traditional story lines; in a rudimentary way, this made them the first playwrights. Aristotle later confirmed that this is what happened, writing in his *Poetics* that drama

began in improvisations [spontaneous creations] . . . originating with the authors of the dithyramb . . . which still survive as institutions in many of our cities. And its advance [evolution into the art of drama] after that was little by little, through their improving on whatever they had before them at each stage. It was in fact only after a long series of changes that the [evolution] of tragedy stopped [after attaining its present] form.[31]

Religious dithyramb was not the only source for Greek drama and theater. Recitations of epic poetry, particularly Homer's *Iliad* and *Odyssey,* also contributed. In the earliest days, traveling poets like Homer stood before an audience and recited the stories, and as time went on these performances became more formal. An important turning point came in 566 B.C., when the Athenians instituted Homeric recitation contests called *rhapsodia,* performed by skilled bards known as *rhapsodes.* No doubt these recitals were accompanied by elaborate gestures and movements, making them an early form of acting.

The World's First Actor

The biggest early step in the evolution of drama and theater occurred in about 534 B.C., when Athens inaugurated an important yearly religious festival, the City Dionysia. As the name suggests, it was held to honor Dionysus, so it was clearly an outgrowth of the earlier ceremonies featuring dithyramb. In fact, the City Dionysia included a dramatic competition involving dithyramb as well as contests among *rhapsodes.*

The overall winner of the competition that year was a man named Thespis. It appears that he was an innovator who introduced some fresh new approaches that transformed the traditional ceremonies into the earliest version of a theatrical play. This play featured most of the standard elements of dithyramb and *rhapsodia.* But it went further by adding to the *rhapsodia* a chorus whose members recited in unison some of the lines and also commented on the events of the story to heighten the dramatic effect. Thespis's other novel idea was to impersonate, rather than just tell about, the story's heroes. In detaching himself from the cho-

rus and playing a character, he became the world's first true actor.

This new way of telling a story immediately caught on with the Athenians, whose approval encouraged Thespis to continue experimenting and expanding the possibilities of the new art form. For example, he

The bard Homer recites his epic poems in this nineteenth-century engraving.

realized that he need not be limited to playing only one character in a story. But how could a single actor differentiate the various characters so that the audience would understand which one was speaking at any given time? His solution was to disguise himself using a series of masks, one for each character; thereafter, masks became a standard convention of Greek theater. "There remains no definitive evidence as to the exact details of such masks," scholar Iris Brook reports.

> The very fact that they originally had to be light enough in weight to be worn by any actor in reasonable comfort [suggests that they were made of perishable materials and] rules out any possibility of their survival. . . . We do know that . . . [they identified] the actor to his audience when he was playing two or more parts and had to make speedy and obvious changes of character. They were also worn by the chorus. . . . From the pictures that have come down to us, it would seem that [the members of] a chorus, more often than not, wore identical masks. [32]

For his invention of masks and other innovations, Thespis became a theater immortal; today, actors are still sometimes referred to as "thespians" in his honor.

The Theater Becomes an Institution

Not much else is known about Thespis. So there is no way to tell how long he remained the dominant figure in Athens's unique new theatrical art form. Other talented and ambitious writer-actors must have competed with him in the City Dionysia, and some of these pioneers survived him. One was Choerilus, who wrote some 160 plays and won the great dramatic competition thirteen times. Another, Pratinas, was said to have composed eighteen tragedies. Nothing else is known about these early theatrical giants.

More certain is where these artists got the ideas for their plays. Greek mythology remained the main source of the characters and plots, along with the *Iliad*, the *Odyssey*, and other epics. In time, though, some playwrights took the then-bold step of depicting important recent historical events. One such innovator was Phrynichus, who caused a controversy at the City Dionysia in 492 B.C. for his play *The Capture of Miletus*, about the fall of that prosperous Greek city to the Persians. According to Herodotus, the play was so moving that "the audience in the theater burst into tears. The author was fined a thousand drachmas for reminding them of a disaster which touched them so closely, and they forbade anybody ever to put the play on the stage again." [33]

By the time that Phrynichus presented this play, the City Dionysia festival had become an ingrained institution, a major holiday attraction eagerly awaited each year by Athenians of all walks of life. It took place over several days at the end of March and was open to all Greeks. Also, any Greek could enter a play in the competition. However, the festival itself, including the actual production of the plays, remained an Athenian

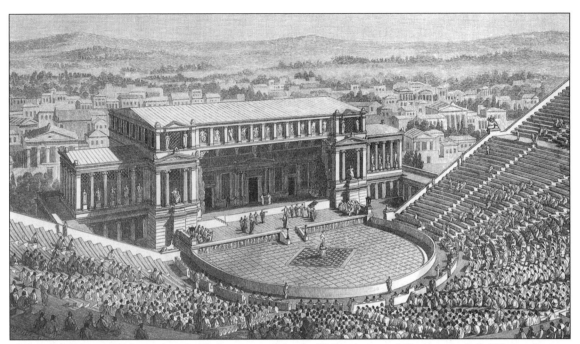

Athens's Theater of Dionysus as it likely appeared in the Hellenistic and Roman periods. The two-story structure is the skene.

monopoly. The Athenian government not only felt the need to control its own public events, but it also desired to use the drama festival as a showcase for the city's growing wealth and cultural achievements. This is why the state financed and maintained the theater building, paid the actors, and provided the prizes for the dramatic contests.

The money for other aspects of play production (costumes, sets, musicians, and the training of the choruses) came from backers, the *choregoi*. The government chose these well-to-do citizens by random drawing and charged them with the duty of supporting the festival. Meanwhile, the playwrights had many duties of their own. In addition to writing the plays, they usually acted in them, rehearsed the choruses, composed the music, choreographed the dances, and supervised all other aspects of production.

Theaters, Scenery, Props, and Special Effects

The playwrights diligently rehearsed their actors and choruses right up to the opening day of the festival. After the spectators had taken their seats in the theater, all of the competing writers and actors, probably accompanied by their respective *choregoi*, entered the theater in a stately parade, marching to the sounds of lyres and other instruments. This theater, the world's first, was appropriately named the Theater of Dionysus. It stood near the southeastern foot of the Acropolis, sat about fourteen thousand spectators, and became the model for the many

In this reconstruction of the Theater of Dionysus, actors perform in the semicircular orchestra. The spectators sit in the theatron.

other Greek theaters erected in the years that followed. The general structural characteristics of such facilities, historian James H. Butler explains,

> consisted of three distinct parts: the *theatron* (viewing place), for spectators; the orchestra (dancing place), where chorus and actors performed; and a later addition, a *skene* (scene building), which provided a scenic backing [and storage for props]. . . . The circular orchestra . . . almost completely surrounded on three sides by the *theatron,* was approximately 65 feet in diameter. On either side of the extremities of the *theatron* . . . was open space for the *parodoi* (entrances into the orchestra) used by chorus members for initial entrances into the playing area, [and] by the actors. . . . In many theaters, the *paradoi* developed subsequently into imposing stone gateways. [34]

In general, these early theater buildings did not use the elaborate painted scenery common in modern stage shows. Instead, the physical settings of the plays were left primarily to the audiences' imaginations. In the Classical Age, the action of the plays usually took place outdoors, in front of a house, palace, temple, or other familiar structure.

The scene building that loomed behind the actors, which the playwright and his crew redecorated as needed, represented the fronts of these buildings. Interiors could not be shown.

Other stage conventions in Greek theaters included the masks and handsome costumes worn by the actors, as well as props. Greek actors tended to use props sparingly. Common ones included statues of gods, couches, torches, chariots, shields and swords, and biers to display dead bodies. In addition, over time various mechanical devices were invented to enhance the atmosphere and provide special effects to wow the audience. One popular device was the *ecclema,* or "tableau machine." Violent acts were almost always committed "indoors," and therefore offstage and out of sight, and the audience learned about them second-hand from messengers or other characters. Sometimes, however, to achieve shock value, a doorway in the *skene* would open and stagehands would push out the *ecclema,* a movable platform on rollers. On the platform, frozen in a dramatic, posed tableau, would be both the murderer and the victim, usually depicted in the seconds immediately following the crime.

Among the other common mechanical devices that developed in Greek theaters were ones meant to represent thunder and flashes of lightning. Used more often, though, was the *machina* (the source of the word machine), a crane with a mechanical arm used to "fly" an actor playing a god or hero through the air above the stage. Over the years, playwrights tended to overuse the *machina* to show gods arriving in the nick of time to tie up the story's loose ends in a simple, neat way. Thus, the term *deus ex machina,* "the god from the machine," eventually became a standard reference to any awkward or unconvincing means used by a playwright to resolve the plot.

Aeschylus, the First Great Tragedian

Of course, the theater building, costumes, props, and special effects were mainly the

Ancient Greek actors try on masks backstage in this reconstruction.

trappings with which to make the central feature—the drama—come to life. The style and quality of the written plays depended on the preferences and sheer talent and skills of the playwrights themselves. The fifth-century B.C. golden age produced four great masters, three of whom specialized in tragedy—the first, and for a long time most prestigious, theatrical style. The three tragedians were Aeschylus, Sophocles, and Euripides. In their view, the core meaning of tragedy was the struggle of human beings to reconcile the existence of both good and evil. As noted scholar Paul Roche puts it:

> The theme of all tragedy is the sadness of life and the universality of evil. The inference the Greeks drew from this was *not* that life was not worth living, but that because it *was* worth living the obstacles to it were worth overcoming. Tragedy is the story of our existence trying to rear its head above the general shambles. The worst and final temptation, no less for us than for an Athenian of the fifth century B.C., is to stop the fight and slide into inactivity of heart and will. [35]

Although early playwrights like Thespis and Phrynichus set the basic form and tone of tragedy, it was the first of the great masters, Aeschylus, who raised the art of tragedy to the level of great literature. Aeschylus was in his thirties or forties when the Persians attacked Greece in the early fifth century B.C. And he fought in the pivotal battles of

Marathon and Salamis. The events surrounding the latter, a huge naval engagement, became the theme of his *Persians,* written in about 472 B.C., the oldest surviving complete tragedy. When, therefore, one reads how the Greeks charged "with courageous hearts to battle," how "ship into ship battered its brazen beak," and how "charge followed charge on every side," the drama is heightened by the realization that it is an actual eyewitness account. The Persian vessels "heeled over," the passage continues,

This drawing of the Athenian playwright Aeschylus is based on a surviving bust.

and "the sea was hidden, carpeted with wrecks and dead men."[36]

Aeschylus followed up the *Persians* with many other plays. Various ancient sources claim he wrote eighty-two in all, but sadly only seven survive complete. Besides the *Persians*, these are *Seven Against Thebes* (467 B.C.); *Agamemnon, The Libation Bearers*, and *The Eumenides* (458); *The Suppliants* (ca. 463); and *Prometheus Bound* (ca. 460). Aeschylus won his first victory in the City Dionysia contests in 484 and went on to win twelve more times.

In addition to being a prolific and major talent, Aeschylus was credited with a crucial theatrical innovation—the introduction of a second actor. Before his time, playwrights made do with one actor, as Thespis had. However, one person can change his mask and reenter from a different door only so many times in one play; so the stories had to be told in simplified form with a limited number of characters. Adding a second actor significantly increased the storytelling potential since it allowed the depiction of twice as many characters.

Sophocles, Master of Characterization

The second Athenian master tragedian, Sophocles, was the most successful dramatist ever to present plays in the Theater of Dionysus. In his first victory in the City Dionysia, in 468 B.C. (for a play titled *Triptolemus*, now lost), he defeated Aeschylus and went on to win first prize at least seventeen more times. Sophocles also wrote more plays than Aeschylus—reportedly 123 in all.

Sophocles, depicted in this statue, reportedly composed 123 plays in all.

Just seven of these have survived. They are, in order of their composition, *Ajax* (ca. 447 B.C.), *Antigone* (ca. 441), *Oedipus the King* (ca. 429), *The Women of Trachis* (ca. 428), *Electra* (ca. 415), *Philoctetes* (ca. 409), and *Oedipus at Colonus* (406).

Sophocles was an expert at characterization—that is, developing the traits and thoughts of the characters to such a degree that they seem like real people. He was also the first playwright to use a third actor (and may also have employed a fourth toward

Oedipus Learns the Hideous Truth

Sophocles' *Oedipus the King,* written in about 429 B.C., has often been called the greatest tragedy ever written. The plot is briefly as follows. Years before the events of the play, Oedipus, a prince of the city of Corinth, heard from an oracle that he would one day kill his father and marry his mother. Hoping to avoid this awful fate, he fled to Thebes, where he eventually became ruler. He married Jocasta, wife of the former king, Laius (who had been killed on a roadside) and had children by her. As the play begins, Thebes is beset by a terrible plague. Creon, Jocasta's brother, consults an oracle, who claims that the gods sent the plague as a punishment for the murder of Jocasta's first husband; the murderer is still at large and must be found and punished before the plague can be averted. Oedipus vows to find and punish this murderer. But soon, the blind prophet Tiresias tells the king that he, Oedipus, is the very culprit whom everyone seeks. At first, Oedipus scoffs at this idea. But soon, he hears his wife discussing the details of her former husband's death. The scene she describes, which took place on a roadside, sounds strangely like an incident in which Oedipus himself had killed a man on his way to Thebes several years earlier. It is not long before a messenger arrives from Corinth and reveals a dark secret. Oedipus is *not* a prince of Corinth but the child of Laius and Jocasta, who abandoned him as an infant. Shepherds had found the baby and taken him to Corinth to be raised. Oedipus now realizes that the man he slew on the roadside was his true father and that he has married his own mother. Devastated by these hideous truths, Jocasta hangs herself and Oedipus gashes out his own eyes and becomes a wandering beggar. As the play ends, Creon assumes the throne of Thebes.

Modern actors employ authentic masks in a production of Sophocles' Oedipus the King.

the end of his career). This further expanded the storytelling powers of drama. The central characters of Sophocles' plays usually display some personal imperfection (often called a "tragic flaw") that causes much suffering as well as their downfalls. The most famous example is Oedipus, king of Thebes in *Oedipus the King*. As the story unfolds, Oedipus's overbearing self-confidence and self-righteousness lead him to discover, to his dismay, that he earlier unknowingly killed his own father and married his own mother. This terrible realization is too much for him to bear, and in a fit of despair he gouges out his eyes.

Yet though Sophocles viewed humans as naturally flawed, he also recognized their many good qualities. As long as they respected the gods and the laws of their communities, there seemed to him no limit to what they might accomplish. He was not alone in this feeling, as revealed in phrases and passages from the works of his fellow dramatists. Surely he spoke for all of them in this famous, stirring passage from *Antigone:*

> Many wonders exist, but none of them are more wonderful than human beings. . . . They have taught themselves to speak and think quickly and to create communities. . . . Clever beyond one's wildest dreams are the abilities that cause them sometimes to do evil and other times to do good. As long as they respect the rule of law and the authority of the gods, their community will proudly continue to thrive. [37]

Euripides and Aristophanes

The third and youngest of the great Athenian tragedians, Euripides, produced his first plays in the City Dionysia in 455 B.C. He wrote perhaps eighty-eight in all, but only nineteen have survived, among them *Alcestis* (438), *Medea* (431), *Hippolytus* (428), *Madness of Heracles* (ca. 420–417), and *The Bacchae* (405). Euripides was a good deal less popular in his own day than either Aeschylus or Sophocles. The main reason for this was that the younger man frequently questioned traditional and widely accepted social values. For example, various passages in Euripides' works imply that the world operates more by chance than under the influence of the gods and preordained fate. Moreover, he often made the gods behave badly in his plays, something rarely seen in the works of his contemporaries. In *Hippolytus,* for example, Aphrodite, goddess of love, savagely strikes out at the title character simply because of her wounded vanity. And in the play *Ion*, the god Apollo rapes and abandons the heroine, who later strongly denounces the deity in a passage that probably shocked many Athenian playgoers.

Euripides also contended that humans have as much right to establish moral values as the gods do. By thus examining how people can shape their own values and destinies, the playwright tended to depict humans and the human condition in highly realistic ways. As a result, to listeners today his dialogue often sounds quite modern and naturalistic.

Equally controversial, though in a different way, was the fourth of the fifth-century B.C. theatrical greats, Aristophanes. Unlike the other three, he specialized in comedy. The exact origins of Greek comedy are unclear, but most scholars think it evolved out of some of the same religious rituals that tragedy did. In some of the early Dionysian ceremonies, the worshippers dressed in animal costumes, particularly those depicting goats and horses. These earthy characters danced, sang, and exchanged off-color jokes with other worshippers. Greek comedy was likely also shaped by mimes, short funny skits that people performed informally in town squares. Eventually actors began writing these skits down, and in time they were staged in theaters, becoming the precursors of full-fledged comic plays.

Aristophanes flourished during the most creative period for Greek comedy, often referred to as the Old Comedy, which lasted from about 450 to 404 B.C. He and his fellow comic playwrights typically presented highly topical humor that poked fun at people of all walks of life. Politicians, generals, and other leaders were particularly favorite targets. This sort of public criticism was possible because of the extraordinary degree of freedom of speech allowed in Athens's democracy, one of the most open in world history. It allowed Aristophanes and his colleagues to incorporate a degree of slapstick humor, dirty language, sexual innuendo, and out-and-out vulgarity that would shock even many modern audiences who are used to watching R-rated movies and cable television.

As for Aristophanes' plays, ancient sources claim he penned forty-four; however, only eleven remain intact. Four of the more famous and often performed in later ages (including today) are *Clouds* (423 B.C.), *Birds* (414), *Lysistrata* (411), and *Frogs* (405). His favorite method was to satirize the leaders and institutions of his day by depicting them in fantastic or absurd situations. In *Clouds*, for instance, the philosopher Socrates is portrayed as a kooky, phony intellectual running a worthless "think-shop"; in *Lysistrata*, city fathers are too pig-headed and arrogant to end a long war, so the women stage a sex strike to force their husbands to make peace; and in *Frogs*, the god Dionysus (representing some arrogant Athenian leaders) is a conceited fool who wants to go to the Underworld and bring back the tragedian Euripides, who recently died.

Greek Drama in Decline

In 404 B.C., only a year after Aristophanes produced *Frogs*, Athens was defeated in the disastrous Peloponnesian War and the golden age of Athenian culture more or less ended. Although the City Dionysia and its theatrical contests continued, the era of extraordinary innovation and enormous creative output ended. Several decades elapsed before a new style of comedy became popular. Called the New Comedy, its heyday was the Hellenistic period, especially from about 330 to 260 B.C.

The leading playwright of the New Comedy was Menander. Of his more than one hundred plays, only one, *The Bad-*

Euripides: All People Are Potentially Equal

One of the accepted social conventions that Euripides boldly questioned was that people in the tradi-
tional aristocratic class were somehow innately better than ordinary folk. The playwright challenged
this notion and advocated judging each indi-
vidual on his own merits in this speech from
his Electra *(translated by Philip Vellacott in*
Euripides: Medea and Other Plays*).*

There is no clear sign to tell the quality of a
man. Nature and place turn vice and virtue
upside down. I've seen a noble father breed
a worthless son, and good sons come of evil
parents; a starved soul housed in a rich man's
palace, a great heart dressed in rags. By what
sign, then, shall one tell good from bad? By
wealth? Wealth's a false standard. By pos-
sessing nothing, then? No; poverty is a dis-
ease; and want itself trains men in crime. Or
must I look to see how men behave in battle? When you're watching your enemy's
spear you don't know who's brave, who's a
coward. The best way is to judge each man
as you find him; there's no rule.

The bold and controversial playwright
Euripides, as depicted in a surviving bust.

Tempered Man, survives complete (though
substantial fragments of *The Samian Women,*
The Arbitration, The Shorn Girl, The Shield,
and a few others exist). Menander and other
New Comedy writers churned out mainly
mannered situation comedies that were generally tamer, less inventive, and less topical
and political than the works of the Old
Comedy. The New Comedy placed common character types in realistic settings and

Sappho's Poems

The vast majority of poets and other writers in ancient Greece were men. One notable exception was Sappho, born in the late seventh century B.C. on the island of Lesbos (off the coast of Asia Minor). Most of her poems are lost, but the one complete poem and more than a hundred fragments of others that have survived provide some information about her life. Judging by these surviving excerpts, her poems seem to have conveyed her personal feelings and emotions with unusual directness, honesty, and sometimes decided intensity. Some also contained erotic qualities and references. This fragment (Josephine Balmer's translation), part of a festive wedding song, is fairly typical of her work:

Lucky bridegroom, the marriage you have prayed for has come to pass and the bride you dreamed of is yours. . . . Beautiful bride, to look at you gives joy; your eyes are like honey, love flows over your gentle face. . . . Aphrodite [goddess of love] has honored you above all others.

Sir Lawrence Alma-Tadema's magnificent painting of Sappho (standing) shows her listening to a fellow poet recite.

followed set formulas. The most popular plotline involved brothers, sisters, lovers, and so on who are long separated but, through a series of comic twists and turns, are reunited in the end. These formulas exerted a strong influence on the writers of prose romances (early novels) in the late Hellenistic and early Roman periods.

In the meantime, during the Hellenistic Age and long afterward, the plays of Aeschylus and the other fifth-century B.C. masters continued to be performed. Most of these were lost forever after the decline of Greco-Roman civilization; and the few that survived were largely forgotten for many centuries. When Europe eventually rediscovered them and they graced theaters once again, they captured the imaginations of new generations, who rightly saw them as timeless expressions of humanity's brightest and darkest attributes.

Athletic
Competitions

At least by the early Archaic Age (ca. 800–700 B.C.), the Greeks had become captivated by participating in or watching athletic competitions. Their word for them was *agon*, meaning a "contest" or "struggle," a term also applied to battles and lawsuits. During the remainder of Archaic times, a significant physical culture (social institutions and customs surrounding physical fitness and athletic training) took root in most Greek communities.

Partly driving this physical culture was the emergence in the late Archaic era and early Classical Age of a new concept that tied athletics and physical fitness directly to one's outlook on life. The Greeks called it *kalokagathia* (from the words *kalos*, meaning "beautiful," and *agathos*, meaning "noble"

or "learned"), roughly translating as the "mind-body ideal." A person who adopted this ideal strove for a combination of physical and intellectual (or moral) excellence in hopes of developing a more rounded and complete personality. At first, *kalokagathia* was fashionable mainly in aristocratic circles since well-to-do and privileged individuals had more leisure time and money than others to spend training and competing. But the rise of democracy in Athens and a number of other Greek states in the Classical era encouraged social equality; in turn, this stimulated the spread of the mind-body ideal to all social classes.

Many Greeks came to glorify a keen mind in a strong, athletic body, therefore. The depth to which this concept became embedded in the popular consciousness is illustrated by a common adage repeated by Herodotus, Plato, and several other Greek writers in describing a backward person: "He can neither read nor swim." [38] Obviously not every Greek possessed the physical and mental ability to achieve the mind-body ideal. But the fact that so many people desired and at least tried to attain it had a profound influence on the development of local social customs and institutions across the Greek world. The gymnasium became an integral feature of the typical Greek town, for instance. In this facility, men of all ages worked out, both to stay in shape and to train for the Olympics and other formal athletic competitions.

Religion, Athletics, and Shared Culture

It is important to emphasize that the Greeks did not view such competitions simply as a

---

The First Recorded Footrace

The first descriptions of athletic competitions in Western literature appear in Homer's Iliad. *In this excerpt from the funeral games of the slain warrior Patroclus (Robert Fagles's translation), the Greek leader Odysseus defeats his colleague, Ajax, in a footrace.*

Ajax shot ahead, with quick Odysseus coming right behind him, close as the weaver's rod to a well-sashed woman's breast . . . so close Odysseus sprinted, hot on Ajax's heels, feet hitting his tracks before the dust could settle and quick Odysseus panting, breathing down his neck, always forcing the pace. . . . In the homestretch, spurting toward the goal, Odysseus prayed in his heart to blazing-eyed Athena, "Hear me, Goddess, help me—hurry, urge me on!" So Odysseus prayed and Athena heard his prayer, put spring in his limbs, his feet. . . . Ajax slipped at a dead run—Athena tripped him up—right where the dung lay slick from bellowing cattle. . . . Dung stuffed his mouth, [and] his nostrils dripped muck as Odysseus flashed past him to come in first by far and carry off the [prize].

A depiction of a footrace on a sixth-century B.C. Athenian vase.

casual pastime meant for relaxation and entertainment. Rather, they saw training for and competing in public games as a very serious matter. One important reason for this was that these events were always staged to honor the gods. In the formative period of Greek religion (in the Dark Age), yearly religious festivals developed in which worshippers marched in formal processions and performed sacrifices of plants and animals. Over time they added musical and athletic contests to these rituals. The athletic competitions came to include several running, jumping, and throwing events (today called track-and-field events) as well as wrestling, boxing, and horse and chariot racing. The athletes solemnly dedicated their creative or physical skills and prowess to whatever god or gods the festival honored.

By the end of the sixth century B.C., four major athletic competitions, each dedicated to an important deity, had emerged on the Greek mainland. They were not simply the most prestigious sporting venues. They were also international (panhellenic, or "all-Greek"), which meant that they attracted athletes and spectators from city-states far and wide. The most distinguished of the four was the Olympic festival, honoring Zeus. It was presented at Olympia every four years. The other three were the Pythian Games, dedicated to Apollo, held at Delphi in the third year after each Olympics; the Isthmian Games, for Poseidon, held every two years at his sanctuary on the Isthmus of Corinth; and the Nemean Games, honoring Zeus, held at two-year intervals at Nemea (a few miles south of Corinth).

These large-scale festivals, in which athletic competitions became the main attraction, constituted what the Greeks called the *periodos,* or "circuit." Although the city-states saw themselves as separate nations, when people from all the states came together periodically in these festivals it naturally produced a culturally unifying effect, in the same way that speaking the same language gave all Greeks a sense of commonality. According to scholar Vera Olivova:

> The sites of the four main games became focal points for the whole Greek world. Amid the fertile variety of the city-states, free of pressure from any central power, it was here that a sense of national identity arose in a purely natural and spontaneous way, through awareness of a high level of shared culture both intellectual and physical, and through a sense of superiority over the slaves and over the neighboring barbarians [non-Greeks]. The outward symbol of this superiority was a strong, tanned, well-developed naked body. It became an ideal for all Greeks, distinguishing them from other peoples, and an object of admiration at all panhellenic festivals. [39]

The Olympic Sanctuary and Truce

Of the four great athletic venues, the Olympic Games was not only the most prestigious but also the oldest. The exact date when Olympia's religious festival and games began is unknown. According to ancient tradition,

Competing in the Nude

No one knows when Greek athletes began competing naked or exactly why the custom developed. What is certain is that nearly all the scenes of sports contests depicted in ancient Greek sculpture and vase paintings show men performing their events in the nude. Yet many people today find it difficult to believe that the athletes, especially runners and wrestlers, did not wear loincloths (like modern athletic supporters) to protect themselves. One recent explanation is that at first they *did* wear such protection and that artists left it out of their depictions as a matter of style—to emphasize the beauty of the nude body. In fact, Homer mentions wrestlers and boxers wearing loincloths in both the *Iliad* and the *Odyssey*. However, the fifth-century B.C. Athenian historian Thucydides claimed that athletes originally wore protection but had discarded it by his day. A number of theories have been proposed for why the athletes discarded clothes and protection. One is that Greek men took pride in their muscular, well-conditioned bodies and wanted to distinguish themselves from and indicate their superiority to "barbarians" (non-Greeks), who preferred to stay clothed in public settings.

they first appeared in 776 B.C. However, archaeologists have found that the site of Olympia was inhabited as far back as the third millennium B.C., early in Greece's Bronze Age, and that some sort of religious observances occurred there from then on. No one knows which gods were originally worshipped. But even after Zeus became the main and permanent focus of worship at Olympia's sacred sanctuary (the Altis), shrines remained honoring various nature gods. Scholars are sure, therefore, that athletic contests took place there well before the traditionally recognized starting date of 776 B.C. So that year likely marks the beginning of the games' ongoing four-year cycle as well as the practice of keeping records of the winners.

Olympia was located within the territory controlled by the city-state of Elis, and at an early date the Eleans took charge of the games held there. The city's elders appointed the *Hellanodikai*, or "Greek judges," who oversaw the athletic events and whose decisions about winners and losers were final. At first, there were two judges. But as the games grew and attracted larger numbers of competitors, more judges were needed. By the early fifth century B.C. there were ten, who were now selected from the Elean citizenry by the drawing of lots. These judges received no pay, as the honor of being chosen was seen as more than adequate compensation. They wore special purple robes, symbolic of their high status. (Purple was

A referee (at right) watches as an athlete prepares to throw the discus. The branch the referee holds was sometimes used to punish rule breakers.

the color traditionally associated with royalty in ancient times.) They wielded so much authority, in fact, that they were allowed to punish rule breakers severely. An athlete caught cheating or taking bribes could be fined, publicly flogged, or—to them most humiliating of all—thrown out of the games, depending on the individual situation.

Officials at Elis were also in charge of announcing the Olympic Games to the Greek world every four years. Three Elean heralds, the *Spondophoroi*, or "Truce Bearers," trav-

eled to every Greek state. Their job was to tell the exact date of the coming games (which varied from one Olympiad to the next), to invite all to attend, and, most important of all, to announce the sacred Olympic truce, or *ekecheiria*. Judith Swaddling, a noted authority on the ancient Olympics, explains:

Originally the Truce lasted for one month, but it was extended to two and then three months, to protect visitors coming from further afield. The terms of the Truce were engraved on a bronze discus which was kept in the Temple of Hera in the Altis. It forbade states participating in the Games to take up arms, to pursue legal disputes, or to carry out death penalties. This was to ensure that pilgrims and athletes traveling to and from Olympia would have a safe journey. Violators of the Truce were heavily fined, and indeed on one occasion, Alexander the Great himself had to recompense [pay damages to] an Athenian who was robbed by some of his mercenaries while traveling to Olympia.[40]

When such travelers reached the sacred Olympic sanctuary, first-time visitors were invariably impressed by its large collection of handsome shrines, temples, athletic facilities, and other structures. Among these was the Temple of Zeus (which housed Phidias's great statue of the god); Zeus's great altar, where the festival's main sacrifices took place; and temples dedicated to Hera (Zeus's wife and protector of marriage), and Rhea (Zeus's mother). There were also several treasuries, each erected by a different city-state, for storing the valuables the pilgrims brought as offerings to the gods. The athletic structures included a stadium for track and field events, a hippodrome (outdoor racetrack) for horse and chariot races, a gymnasium, and some public baths. The sanctuaries at Nemea, Delphi, and Isthmia featured similar groups of structures, although on a somewhat smaller scale.

The Program of Events

Not everyone made it to the Olympic sanctuary at the same time. The athletes were required to arrive in Elis at least a month early so they could train under the supervision of Elean officials. In the weeks that followed, the spectators came in increasing numbers and set up tents and makeshift huts in fields surrounding the sanctuary. They were accompanied by legions of vendors, prostitutes, gamblers, and others hoping to

The Temple of Zeus (right) and other buildings at Olympia are reconstructed in this drawing. The site also featured thousands of statues.

make a fast buck off the gathered crowds. According to a first-century A.D. description of the crowds at Isthmia:

> Writers were reading their rubbish aloud. Many poets were reciting their verses to the applause of others, many conjurers [magicians] were showing off their tricks, [and] fortune-tellers theirs. There were countless advocates [lawyers] perverting the law and not a few peddlers hawking everything and anything.[41]

The program of events at Olympia took place over the course of five days. On the first day, the athletes swore an oath in the Bouleuterion (Council Chamber), a building situated not far south of the Temple of Zeus. Pausanias records that the oaths were recited to an outdoor statue of Zeus:

> Tradition dictates that the athletes and their fathers and brothers and even their trainers should take before this statue an oath . . . to do no wrong to the Olympic Games. The actual athletes have to swear further that they have been in full training for ten months.[42]

Pausanias also says that the judges swore to be fair, to refrain from taking bribes, and to keep secret anything they had learned about the athletes during the training period. The rest of the first day was devoted to private and public prayers, public sacrifices, the consulting of holy oracles, and orations by philosophers, historians, and others.

On the second day of the festival, in the morning, the horse and chariot races took place in the hippodrome. In the afternoon, the pentathlon (which combined running, jumping, the discus throw, the javelin throw, and wrestling) was held. And in the evening, the participants enjoyed feasts and sang victory hymns.

The third day (which had been planned ahead to coincide with the full moon) witnessed the main religious observances. In the morning, a great procession marched to Zeus's outdoor altar (located about two hundred feet north of the god's temple). There, a hundred oxen were sacrificed in a grand ceremony. According to Pausanias:

> The first step of the altar is 125 feet in circumference and is called the "Outer Circle." The step above the Outer Circle is 32 feet in circumference. The total height of the altar is 22 feet. The rule is to kill the animals in the lower part of the Outer Circle and then to carry the thighs to the top of the altar and burn them there as a sacrifice.[43]

After the conclusion of these sacrifices, the boys' competitions (for youths between the ages of twelve and eighteen) took place. And after the sun went down, large numbers of worshippers feasted on the cooked meat of the oxen that had been sacrificed earlier.

On the fourth day, the footraces and combat sports were held. The combat events included wrestling, boxing, and the *pankration,* a forceful combination of both wrestling and boxing moves. Finally, the fifth day was

Worshippers lead a cow to an altar, where they will sacrifice the animal to the goddess Athena (represented at right), in a painting on a storage jar.

devoted to crowning the winners of the various events, followed by more sacrifices, feasts, and other celebrations.

Formal and Informal Wrestling Bouts

All of the events held in the course of the games were popular. And it is difficult to tell which, if any, was categorically the most popular. However, wrestling would be a reasonable educated guess. The fact is that the Greeks viewed wrestling training as the most crucial component of physical education. Also, Greek boys participated in informal wrestling bouts in the same manner that modern American and European boys play backlot football or soccer; and grown men enjoyed friendly wrestling matches as much as they did entertaining friends or discussing politics. Wrestling was so integral to Greek life that by the fifth century B.C. almost every Greek town had a *palaestra*, a wrestling facility or a section of a gymnasium devoted to wrestling.

The Greeks engaged in two general types of wrestling—"upright" and "ground." Both began with the fighters in a standing position. The difference was that in upright wrestling, which was the only version allowed in formal competitions, the main object was

Two wrestlers grapple while a referee looks on. Evidence suggests that wrestlers often resorted to rough tactics, such as choking and breaking fingers.

to throw one's opponent to the ground. This constituted a fall (compared to modern amateur wrestling, in which holding an opponent's shoulders to the mat—called pinning—gains a fall). Winning required scoring three falls, so a victor was called a *triakter,* or "tripler." In ground wrestling, practiced mainly in the *palaestra,* after a successful throw the fighters continued to struggle on the ground until one raised his hand, the signal that he submitted.

Modern scholars are somewhat unclear about the rules that applied to upright wrestling matches in formal competitions like the Olympics. But they have pieced together a fairly clear picture. Tripping seems to have been allowed, but evidence suggests that leg holds were either prohibited or rarely used. Punching and eye gouging were banned, as they are in modern amateur wrestling. In addition, archaeologists have found a decree (excavated at Olympia) stating that a wrestler could not break his opponent's fingers.

Wrestlers who did not adhere to these sanctions suffered the wrath of the Elean judges, who acted as referees and brandished large rods with which to whack rule breakers. Such punishments must have been fairly common. Evidence shows that the wrestlers at the major athletic competitions fought hard and often resorted to brutal tactics to ensure victory. Employing dangerous strangleholds was not unusual, for instance. And in spite of the rule against breaking fingers, in the mid–fifth century B.C. a Sicilian Greek named Leontiskos twice won the Olympic wrestling using this very tactic. Centuries later Pausanias saw Leontiskos's statue at Olympia. It stood beside that of a *pankrationist* named Sostratos, who broke so many of his opponent's fingers that he became known as "Mr. Fingertips."

Local Competitions

In addition to the Olympics and the other "big four" Greek athletic venues, there were numerous local competitions held by individual city-states. The largest and most prestigious of these were the games staged at Athens and associated with the great religious festival known as the Panathenaea (meaning "All the Athenians"). It took place once a year but was mounted on a much grander scale every four years. During most of the Classical Age, the Panathenaic contests were held in the city's marketplace and, like the circuit games, drew spectators from across the Greek world.

The events of the Athenian games fell into two broad categories. The first included the standard ones that were also featured in the circuit games, such as running, jumping, throwing the discus, wrestling, boxing, and chariot racing. These were generally open to non-Athenians as well as Athenians.

The second major category of Panathenaic contests included the events that were open only to Athenian citizens. Among these were some military-style horse-related events that did not appear in the Olympics and other circuit games. One, whose details remain obscure, was a sort of parade for two-horse chariots in which the teams were likely judged on their ability to march and drill in a precise manner. Another Athenian equestrian event featured galloping horses whose riders threw javelins at targets.

Another group of Panathenaic events that were open only to Athenians were the tribal contests. (Like other Greek states, Athens had several traditional tribes, large kinship groups, each made up of a number of clans and families related by blood.) One of the more popular of the tribal events was the "Pyrrhic dance." According to tradition, the goddess Athena herself had performed it first, directly after she had emerged, fully grown

Greek athletes perform in graceful unison in Sir Lawrence Alma-Tadema's painting of the Pyrrhic dance.

and armored, from the head of her divine father, Zeus. Painted and sculpted depictions suggest that each tribe entered a team of men who carried spears and shields but who were otherwise nude. These contestants went through a complex and vigorous series of precision moves in unison. "The warrior dance," Plato writes, which is

> rightly termed Pyrrhic ["fiery"] . . . imitates the modes of avoiding blows and missiles by dropping or giving way, or springing aside, or rising up or falling down; [it] also . . . [features] the imitation of archery and the hurling of javelins, and all sorts of blows. [44]

Tribal torch races, for both individuals and teams, were also popular in Athens's Panathenaic games. The team event was a relay race in which each team had up to forty runners. Each man ran about two hundred feet and then passed a lit torch to a teammate, who also sprinted two hundred feet, and so on for a total distance of a little over a mile and a half. As for the solo torch races, Pausanias describes one he witnessed himself. The runners, he says, started outside the city limits at an altar dedicated to Prometheus, the legendary god who gave fire to humans, and ended up in the marketplace: "The contest consists of running while keeping the torch alight; if the first man's torch is out he loses and the second man wins; if his is not burning either, the third man wins; if all the torches are out, no one wins." [45] In a solo race in which there was a clear winner, he had the honor of

using his torch to light the festival's sacrificial altar. (The organizers of the modern Olympic Games borrowed this idea by having a lone runner carry a torch around the stadium and light the symbolic Olympic flame. But no such ceremony, nor any other event involving torches, took place at the ancient Olympics.)

The Drive to Win

The Greeks devoted so much energy and enthusiasm to athletic competitions like the Panathenaea and the Olympic Games that at first glance one might assume they were motivated mainly by the love of sport. In fact, modern scholars long thought that Greek athletes began as "gentleman amateurs" who received no monetary awards and competed mainly out of a "noble" spirit of athletic comradeship. This supposition was based on the fact that winners at the Olympics and other circuit games were awarded simple crowns fashioned from leaves.

Scholars now know that this theory is erroneous. The truth is that the modern concept of amateur athletics did not exist in ancient Greece. Crowns of leaves were indeed the sole prizes awarded at the circuit games, but many athletes received financial support behind the scenes from well-to-do patrons.

Also, victorious competitors always garnered numerous financial and other awards when they returned to their home cities. These awards included bronze tripods, ornamental cups, and jars of olive oil, which the athletes could sell for a profit. Such prizes were often generous and quite valuable. In Athens in the late fifth century B.C., for instance, a victorious runner at the Panathenaea was awarded one hundred jars of olive oil, which had a total worth of about twelve hundred drachmas. An average Greek worker in that era earned about one drachma per day (or about three hundred drachmas per year). So a runner might receive the equivalent of four years' salary by winning a single footrace.

Moreover, Athens was one of a number of Greek city-states that provided free meals for life to native sons who had been victorious in the circuit games. And all of the hundreds of local games across Greece featured the custom of distributing cash prizes to winning athletes. Last but not least, the most successful athletes were glorified by having choral odes composed for them or statues carved in their likenesses.

Thus, the idea of competing mainly out of simple love of sport and the desire to share good fellowship with other athletes, win or lose, is strictly a modern concept. Indeed, winning was so important to ancient Greek athletes that losers often suffered shame. Four losers at the Pythian Games, Pindar writes, received "no glad homecoming." Instead, "when they meet their mothers, [these young men] have no sweet laughter

The Mystery of the Ancient Long Jump

The ancient Greek broad jump, or long jump, remains a bit of an enigma to modern historians, mainly because the jumps recorded by ancient writers are much too long to be believed. The modern world record for the long jump is just under thirty feet. Yet Phayllus of Kroton, a military hero and renowned athlete, was said to have jumped fifty-five feet. And a competitor named Chionis of Sparta supposedly leaped fifty-two feet. Even factoring in the small hand weights these jumpers used, which gave them a slight extra boost, it seems physically impossible for them to have exceeded today's best jumpers by more than twenty feet. The following are a few potential explanations for this discrepancy: the ancient texts are in error; the Greeks were physically superior to modern people; the hand weights were even more efficient than shown in modern experiments; the "feet" used to measure ancient jumps were much shorter than the modern foot; the ancient jump was actually a multiple jump, similar to the modern triple jump (or "hop, skip, and jump"). A majority of scholars presently favor the last option—a multiple jump. This is supported by the fact that the modern record for the triple jump (about fifty-eight feet) is in the same range as records for the ancient long jump.

Victorious athletes stand before the Olympic judges to receive their crowns of leaves in this eighteenth-century English painting.

to cheer them up. . . . In back streets they cower, avoiding their enemies. Disaster has bitten them."[46] Unlike modern athletes, therefore, who compete against the clock or measuring tape in an effort to set records, Greek athletes cared only about defeating their opponents and capturing first place.

This attitude toward athletic contests also derived from a deep-seated and intense desire within the Greek psyche to be the best (*aristos*) in a given endeavor. Such competitions, as scholar David C. Young puts it, were part of "the general Greek struggle to rise above man's essentially ephemeral [impermanent], abject condition and do

what a man cannot ordinarily do." In the athletic stadium, there were no distinctions of class or wealth. All opponents met as equals, so a person of humble status could make his mark. "In that quest for distinction through excellence," Young continues,

we find the driving force behind Greek athletics . . . more even than in the money to be made from so lucrative a business. And in the readiness of adult men to run the naked risk of public dishonor for the chance to achieve distinction . . . we find what separated the Greeks out from other people.[47]

Leisure Activities and Games

Every culture in every age has had its leisure activities, often including different kinds of activities appealing to various social classes, age groups, genders, and so on. In the case of the ancient Greeks, leisure life and playing games occupied a particularly important societal niche. This was partly because growing food, making a living, dealing with disability and sickness, and other realities of everyday life were so difficult, time-consuming, and in general no laughing matter. So people needed a periodic release through relaxation and play. Other, less tangible factors unique to Greece's geography, climate, and earliest cultural customs seem also to have contributed to the Greek love and exploitation of leisure. In her classic study of the Greek mind-set, *The Greek Way*, the late and noted scholar Edith Hamilton suggests that

> somewhere among those steep stone mountains, in little sheltered valleys where the great hills were ramparts to defend and men could have security for peace and happy living . . . the joy of life found expression. Perhaps it was born there, among the shepherds pasturing their flocks where the wild flowers made a glory on the hillside; among the sailors on a sapphire sea washing enchanted islands purple in a luminous air.[48]

The first Greek games that come to mind, of course, are the formal athletic contests held at Olympia and elsewhere across Greece.

Dozens of separate events, from running, to throwing, to riding, to wrestling were included. There was also the formal venue of the theater, where large crowds gathered to watch scripted tragedies and comedies unfold. Yet like people today, the Greeks also had many less formal games and leisure activities that they pursued at home, in gymnasiums, in the streets, and in fields. These included dinner and drinking parties, playing and listening to music, singing and dancing, hunting and fishing, playing ball, gambling, and many more. The Greeks "played on a great scale," Hamilton notes, and

> if we had no other knowledge of what the Greeks were like, if nothing were left

of Greek art and literature, the fact that they were in love with play and played magnificently would be proof enough of how they lived and how they looked at life. . . . To rejoice in life, to find the world beautiful and delightful to live in, was a mark of the Greek spirit.[49]

Private Banquets

Hamilton's lyrical description of the Greek love of play, though essentially accurate, does leave out one salient point. Namely, Greek men benefited considerably more from play and leisure activity than Greek women. This is because Greek society was strictly male dominated. And women usually (with some exceptions in certain times and places) led

In this painting from an ancient vase (the so-called "Vase of Darius"), a man plays a board game. The Greeks enjoyed playing many different kinds of games.

A painting from the bottom of a drinking cup shows men reclining on couches at a symposium, or private drinking party, as a flute player entertains.

sheltered, sometimes secluded lives. Women were not allowed to act on the stage, for example; men played all the women's parts. Similarly, women could not participate in the Olympic Games and for a number of centuries were not even allowed to be spectators.

One widely popular leisure activity that the Greeks particularly viewed as the exclusive domain of men was the private banquet, usually followed by a symposium, or after-dinner drinking party. The average Greek townhouse had a dining room or area for occasions when the family members, male and female, ate together. But in addition, the man of the house (the husband, father, grown son, or whomever) had his own private dining room, called the *andron*. This is where he entertained his male guests. And his wife, mother, daughters, and other women under his roof were not allowed in or near this chamber when it was in use. (The men in a typical Greek family were very cautious about allowing their wives and daughters to speak and socialize with men from outside the extended family. The attitude stemmed partly from the belief that women were weak willed and would not be able to stop attempts by strange men to seduce them.)

Following custom, the guests who attended such parties bathed first and put on fresh clothes. Most Greeks were very concerned about their outward appearance, especially in formal situations, which dinner parties were considered to be. Upon entering the host's home, the men removed their shoes. (The streets were often muddy and/or littered with animal manure and other refuse; taking off one's shoes helped to keep the interior of the house cleaner longer.) If the host had slaves, they washed the guests' feet and led them into the *andron*, where the host greeted them.

The same slaves served the meal (except in a few wealthy households, which had butlers to greet the guests and kitchen workers to serve the meals.) They brought the food in bowls, which rested on small portable tables. These tables were set up near couches on which the guests reclined, with their upper bodies propped up on their elbows or on pillows. Proper etiquette dictated that the most honored guest (or guests) sat nearest the host. Most food was eaten with the hands, except for soup, pudding, and so on, for which spoons were supplied. It was also customary to wipe one's fingers on a piece of bread, as no formal table napkins existed yet; and people threw their chicken bones, cherry pits, and other scraps on the floor. The family dogs cleared away part of this mess and the slaves cleaned up what was left the next morning.

Drinking Parties

After the meal, the drinking began. Wine was the main drink, diluted with water in a container designed specifically for that purpose. It was common for the guests to drink to excess, a fact made clear in the writings of a number of ancient authors. In one of his more famous dialogues, with the appropriate title of the *Symposium,* Plato describes

a party attended by some Athenian men, among them his mentor, Socrates. The members of the group had gotten roaring drunk at a similar party the night before and were badly hung over. As a result, they decided not to overdo it at the present party.

This did not ruin the occasion, for the men who attended symposia had a number of other ways to enjoy themselves. They told stories, posed riddles, engaged in word games, sang songs, and played games.

One of the more popular games was *cottabos*. The object was to toss the wine dregs from the bottoms of one's cup at a guest's cup, a bowl, a vase resting on a pedestal, or at some other target. Robert Flaceliere describes another variation of the game:

> The bowl which formed the target might be filled with water, and a number of tiny clay saucers set afloat in it. The game then consisted in aiming at these miniscule [very small] "boats" and throwing the wine so skillfully that it made them overturn and sink. The *cottabos* prize went to whoever caused the largest number of "shipwrecks."[50]

In addition to entertaining themselves, the guests often enjoyed the offerings of live entertainers hired by the host. Among these were *hetairai*, high-class, well-educated prostitutes who engaged the men in conversation as well as provided them with sex. They were mostly foreigners (at least in Athens, from which most of the evidence for them comes) who commanded high fees. As scholar Eva Cantarella explains, the lure of the *hetaira* for an educated Greek man was that she provided him with more than just sex, a nicety he could get at any time from his wife or slave:

> The *hetaira* was a sort of remedy provided by a society of men which, having segregated its women, still considered that the company of some of them could enliven their social activities, meetings among friends, and discussions which their wives, even if they had been allowed to take part, would not have been able to sustain. Enter the *hetaira*, who was paid for a relationship (including sex) which was neither exclusive nor merely occasional, as indicated by her name, which means "companion." This relationship was meant to be somehow gratifying to the man, even on the intellectual level, and was thus completely different from men's relationships with either wives or [ordinary] prostitutes. [51]

Other kinds of entertainers at private parties included musicians, dancers, and acrobats. In his own work titled the *Symposium*, Xenophon describes such entertainers at a party:

> A Syracusan [a native of the Greek city of Syracuse, on the Italian island of

This painting on the bottom of a red-figure cup, dated to ca. 480 B.C., depicts young men playing the parlor game cottabos *at a symposium.*

Sicily] came to provide entertainment. He had with him a girl who was an expert pipe player, another who was an acrobatic dancer, and a very attractive boy who both played the lyre and danced extremely well. . . . A man standing by the dancer handed her hoops until she had twelve. She took them and threw them spinning up into the air as she danced, judging how high to throw them so as to catch them in time for the music. . . . Next, a circular frame was brought in, closely set around with upright sword-blades and the dancer turned somersaults into this and out again over the blades, so that the spectators were afraid that she would hurt herself; but she went through her performance confidently and safely.[52]

Music and Dancing

Xenophon's mention of musicians at a party is not surprising. Music played an integral role in numerous aspects of Greek life, and it would not be a stereotype or exaggeration to say that the ancient Greeks were a highly musical people. Music was played in weddings and funerals, religious celebrations, the theater, the schools, athletic and musical competitions, and even on the battlefield.

The most popular instruments played at these venues were the lyre, *kithara*, and *aulos*. The lyre was a small harp that the player held on his or her lap. The *kithara*, also a stringed instrument but a good deal larger, forcing the musician to stand, was played by plucking the strings with a small pick called a plectrum. The *aulos* was a woodwind instrument. Because it employed a thin reed that vibrated when the player blew on it, it was similar to the modern oboe and clarinet (though it is now often misleadingly called a flute). "The *aulos* was sometimes a single pipe," scholar Waldo E. Sweet points out,

but the common form had two pipes and was called a *diaulos*. . . . The pipes

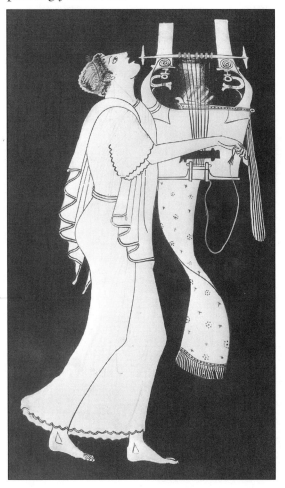

A woman plays a stringed instrument in this painting from a vase.

The Gifted Aspasia

Of the high-class, educated prostitutes (hetairai) *who entertained men at dinner parties, one of the smartest, and certainly the most famous, was Aspasia. Born in Miletus, she traveled to Athens and there became mistress to Pericles, the leading Greek statesman of the fifth century* B.C. *After he divorced his wife, Aspasia moved in with him and they remained together until his death in 429* B.C. *They had a child together and by all accounts shared much genuine love and respect. According to Plutarch in his biography of Pericles (in Ian Scott-Kilvert's* Rise and Fall of Athens*):*

Aspasia, mistress of the Athenian leader Pericles, was famous for her charm and wit.

[Pericles] was attracted to Aspasia mainly because of her rare political wisdom . . . [and his] attachment to [her] seems to have been a . . . passionate affair. [After his divorce] when they [he and his wife] found each other incompatible, Pericles legally handed her over to another man with her own consent and himself lived with Aspasia, whom he loved dearly. . . . Every day, when he went out to the marketplace and returned, he greeted her with a kiss.

were usually held together by a strap . . . a device that assisted the player in blowing evenly. The number of holes in the pipes varied from six to sixteen . . . which the player covered and uncovered with the fingers to produce different notes. [53]

Because most Greek men learned to play the lyre in school, they could entertain themselves and others at parties and in other settings. The most talented musicians in a family likely played at weddings, birth celebrations, clan gatherings, and so forth. And as seen in Xenophon's description of

A painting on a red-figure krater *(a container for mixing wine and water) dating from ca. 510 B.C. shows men competing in a musical contest.*

a symposium, expert musicians were frequently hired for various occasions. Some of the more accomplished players took part in the public athletic competitions, and not just during the religious and other ceremonial moments. Numerous vase paintings dating from the sixth century onward show *aulos* players providing musical accompaniment to the athletes as they ran, jumped, threw, boxed, and wrestled.

Moreover, the victory odes composed for the winners of these events were played by ensembles of musicians backed up by choirs of singers. The words to a number of Pindar's odes have survived, though sadly the tunes to which these lyrics were set are lost. Like the athletes, the musicians had their own competitions, the most prestigious of which took place at the Pythian Games at Delphi. (This

is probably because Apollo, Delphi's principal deity, was the patron of music and musicians as well as god of prophecy and truth.) Fortunately, an ode Pindar composed for a victorious musician named Midas has survived. It reads in part:

I pray you, lover of splendor, fairest of mortal cities. . . . Take this Pythian [victory] wreath achieved by glorious Midas, and take himself, victor of Greece, in that art [of music] which [the goddess] Athena invented . . . and gave her invention to mortal men, naming it, "The Many-Headed Tune," the glorious summons to the multitudinous games, blown through thin bronze, and blown through the reeds which grow near the fair-spaced city of the Graces.[54]

Other varieties and categories of music included drinking songs, dirges sung in funeral marches, rhythmic chants sung in religious processions, songs of praise, songs chanted by the choruses in theatrical plays, and battle hymns sung by soldiers marching toward the enemy. In his *Persians,* the playwright Aeschylus describes the Greek sailors singing as they bore down on the Persian ships in the battle of Salamis: "From the Greek ships rose like a song of joy the piercing battle-cry." Greeks standing on the shore to witness the battle then took up the tune: "And from the island crags echoed an answering shout." It is not surprising that the sound of tens of thousands of voices raised in enthusiastic song disquieted the enemy fighters, who were not used to such displays: "The Persians knew their error; fear gripped every man. They were no fugitives who sang that terrifying battle hymn, but Greeks charging with courageous hearts to battle." [55]

Greek music often provided accompaniment for dancing. The Greeks had dances to fit many occasions, including weddings, religious celebrations, harvest time, baby-naming ceremonies, theatrical plays, banquets, and so on. Many of these dances had colorful names: "Setting the World on Fire," "The Itch," "The Piglet," "The Snort," "Stealing the Meat," and "Knocking at the Door," to name only a few. Alas, no one knows exactly how any of these dances were performed. A mere approximation of the moves of a popular Spartan dance has survived in one of Lucian's works:

The so-called Necklace Dance . . . is a dance of boys and girls mixed, who move in single file and really do resemble a necklace. The young man goes ahead, dancing with abandon and using movements which he will someday use in battle, and the girl follows, demonstrating how to dance the feminine role with restraint, and so the Necklace alternates modesty with manliness. [56]

Hunting

Dancing was undoubtedly one of the most ancient of leisure pastimes, but hunting was likely even older. In the earliest times—before and during the Bronze Age—hunting was doubtless viewed less often as a sporting activity and more often as a necessary way to get food and/or protect one's family and community from wild beasts. Lions and wild boars still roamed mainland Greece in the Bronze Age; and packs of wolves persisted in the hills well into the Classical Age. One of the most famous scenes in Homer's *Odyssey* describes the hero Odysseus grappling with a fierce wild boar. The passage reads in part:

With bristling back and eyes aflame, [the boar] faced the hunters. Odysseus was the first to act. Poising his long spear in his great hand, he rushed in, eager to score a hit. But the boar was too quick and caught him above the knee, where he gave him a long flesh-wound with a cross lunge of his tusk. [57]

In the Archaic, Classical, and Hellenistic periods, some people still hunted for food. But a fair number, especially the well-to-do, who could afford horses, hunting dogs, and elaborate traps, engaged in hunts more for the challenge and fun of it. Hunters used bows and arrows, slings, spears, hatchets, knives, nets, and even clubs and sticks, depending on the prey and situation. Trapping was the most prevalent method. For this, various traps were devised, including a spring trap described by Xenophon that was effective at catching deer. There were also pit traps. "A deep pit was dug," Flaceliere explains,

> with sheer sides, and then branches and leaves were laid across it by way of camouflage. In the middle, an upright stake was rigged, with a lamb tethered to it. The lamb's bleatings attracted the carnivore, the branches gave way under its weight, and it crashed through to the bottom of the pit. In order to get it up, an open cage was lowered into the bottom of the pit, with a hunk of meat inside it. The moment the animal entered the cage, the door was dropped shut and the cage hauled up again. [58]

Mountain Climbing

Like hunting, mountain climbing is a leisure activity associated with nature and the great outdoors. As a rule, most Greeks did not climb mountains just for the fun of it, however. Greece is very mountainous, and its ancient inhabitants were forced to scale rugged hillsides on a regular basis just to tend their sheep or travel to a neighboring village. In a wry passage, Sweet quips that the Greeks considered the mountains an abominable mistake of nature . . . [and] no one was inspired to comment on the beauty of the mountains. Very few ancients climbed a mountain "because it was there," as the modern cliché has it. If one did climb a peak, it was by the easiest route. There is no evidence that there were ascents where the climber deliberately chose the most difficult route. [59]

Still, a few Greeks did climb mountains to enjoy the splendid view from the top. Some evidence suggests that this pastime did not become prevalent until the Roman period, when Rome's government provided comforts for climbers and hikers on a few notable peaks. The first-century B.C. Greek traveler Strabo said that Mt. Etna, the great volcano in Sicily, had lookouts, huts with sleeping accommodations, and other such facilities. In fact, he claimed, Etna became a popular tourist attraction for people from across the Mediterranean world, including many Greeks:

> Near the town of Centoripa is a small village called Etna, which takes in climbers and sends them on their way, for the ridge of the mountain begins here. Those who had recently climbed the summit told me that at the top was a level plain. . . . Two of their party were courageous enough to venture into the plain of this crater, but since the sand on which they were walking was becoming hotter and deeper, they turned back. [60]

A Hunter Fights a Wild Boar

This translation of the famous fight between Odysseus and the wild boar from Homer's Odyssey *is by the late E.V. Rieu.*

[On] the steep and wooded heights of Mt. Parnassus . . . the hounds, hot on the scent, preceded [the hunters]. Behind came . . . good Odysseus, close up on the pack and swinging his long spear. It was at this spot that a mighty boar had its lair, in a thicket so dense that when the winds blew moist not a breath could get inside. . . . The boar heard the footfalls of the men and hounds as they pressed forward in the chase. He sallied out from his den and with bristling back and eyes aflame, he faced the hunters. Odysseus was the first to act. Poising his long spear in his great hand, he rushed in, eager to score a hit. But the boar was too quick and caught him above the knee, where he gave him a long flesh-wound with a cross lunge of his tusk, but failed to reach the bone. Odysseus's thrust went home as well. He struck him on the right shoulder, and the point of his bright spear transfixed [ran through] the boar, who sank to earth with a grunt and there gave up his life.

An old engraving shows the young Odysseus fighting the wild boar.

Playing Ball

Much less dangerous but still challenging were ball games, of which many different types existed in the Greek lands. One seems to have involved a participant trying to hang on to a ball while other players tried to take it away. The game was rough, though, because it allowed the participants to employ headlocks and other wrestling holds. The renowned Greek doctor Galen advocated it as a way to stay in shape, writing that it was the only game

which is so democratic that anyone, no matter how small his income, can take part. You need no nets, no weapons, no horses, no hounds—just a single ball, and a small one at that. . . . The capacity . . . to move all the parts of the body equally . . . is something found in no other exercise except that with a small ball. . . . When for example, people face each other, vigorously attempting to prevent each another from taking the space between, the exercise is a very heavy, vigorous one, involving much use of the hold by the neck, and many wrestling holds. . . . The loins and legs

are also subject to great strain in this kind of activity; it requires great steadiness on one's feet.[61]

This game may have been an informal and nonteam variety of one of the most popular of all ancient ball games, a team sport the Greeks called *phaininda* (and the Romans *harpastum*). The second-century A.D. Greek writer Athenaeus provides this sketchy overview of the game:

He seized the ball and passed it with a laugh to one, while the other player he dodged; from one he pushed it out of the way, while he raised another player to his feet amid resounding shouts of "Out of bounds," "Too far," "Right beside him," "Over his head,"

In this carved bas-relief, Greek athletes face off in a ball game that seems to have been similar to modern field hockey.

Another bas-relief shows six men playing a ball game. Their posture and moves suggest it was a field sport akin to modern rugby or soccer.

"On the ground," "Up in the air," "Too short," "Pass it back." [62]

Judging by this passage, *phaininda* may have been somewhat similar to modern rugby, which itself was the rough model for American football. Some scholars disagree with this proposal and suggest instead that another ancient team game, *episkyros,* was closer to rugby. As evidence, they cite the following tract by the second-century A.D. Greek scholar Julius Pollux:

This [game] is played by [two] teams of equal numbers standing opposite one another. They mark out a line between them with stone chips; this is the *skyros* [scrimmage line?], on which the ball is placed. They then mark out two other lines, one behind each team [goal lines?]. The team which secures possession of the ball throws it over their opponents, who then try to get hold of the ball and throw it back, until one side pushes the other over the line behind them. The game might be called a Ball Battle. [63]

It is possible that *phaininda* and *episkyros* were simply variations of the same game, each with its own unique moves and rules, as in the case of modern rugby and football.

What is more certain is that, no matter how busy they were, the Greeks made time for such games and leisure activities. And in response to the many harsh and grim realities of life in the ancient world, they embraced the more joyful and comfortable aspects with eagerness and passion. A character in Homer's *Odyssey* surely spoke for all Greeks when he said, "The things in which we take a perennial delight are the feast, the lyre, the dance, clean linen in plenty, a hot bath, and our beds." [64]

Notes

Introduction: From Ideal to Real: Evolving Views of Greek Culture

1. Grigorios Paliouritis, *Archaiologia Elliniki,* quoted in Richard Clogg, *A Concise History of Greece.* New York: Cambridge University Press, 1992, p. 28.
2. Quoted in Charles Freeman, *The Greek Achievement: The Foundation of the Western World.* New York: Viking, 1999, p. 6.
3. Freeman, *The Greek Achievement,* p. 13.

Chapter 1: Monumental and Public Architecture

4. Thucydides, *The Peloponnesian War,* trans. Rex Warner. New York: Penguin, 1972, p. 41.
5. Quoted in Thucydides, *The Peloponnesian War,* pp. 147–49.
6. Quoted in Thucydides, *The Peloponnesian War,* p. 148.
7. Plutarch, *Life of Pericles,* in *The Rise and Fall of Athens: Nine Greek Lives by Plutarch,* trans. Ian Scott-Kilvert. New York: Penguin, 1960, p. 177.
8. Chester G. Starr, *A History of the Ancient World.* New York: Oxford University Press, 1991, p. 107.

9. William R. Biers, *The Archaeology of Greece.* Ithaca, NY: Cornell University Press, 1996, p. 70.
10. A.W. Lawrence, *Greek Architecture,* rev. R.A. Tomlinson. New Haven, CT: Yale University Press, 1996, p. 190.

Chapter 2: Sculpture, Painting, and Ceramics

11. Quoted in J.J. Pollitt, ed. and trans., *The Art of Ancient Greece: Sources and Documents.* New York: Cambridge University Press, 1990, p. 12.
12. Biers, *The Archaeology of Greece,* pp. 44–45.
13. Chester G. Starr, *The Ancient Greeks.* New York: Oxford University Press, 1971, p. 132.
14. Thomas Craven, *The Pocket Book of Greek Art.* New York: Pocket, 1950, p. 37.
15. Pausanias, *Guide to Greece,* vol. 1, trans. Peter Levi. New York: Penguin, 1971, pp. 69–70.
16. Quoted in Pollitt, *The Art of Ancient Greece,* pp. 61–62.
17. Robert B. Kebric, *Greek People.* Mountain View, CA: Mayfield, 2001, p. 132.
18. Pausanius, *Guide to Greece,* vol. 1, pp. 469–71.

19. Biers, *The Archaeology of Greece*, pp. 286, 303.

20. Biers, *The Archaeology of Greece*, p. 286.

21. Robert Flaceliere, *Daily Life in Greece at the Time of Pericles*, trans. Peter Green. London: Phoenix, 1996, p. 132.

Chapter 3: Literature and the Pursuit of Knowledge

22. Lesley Adkins and Roy A. Adkins, *Handbook to Life in Ancient Greece*. New York: Facts On File, 1997, p. 241.

23. Robert Flaceliere, *A Literary History of Greece*, trans. Douglas Garman. Chicago: Aldine, 1964, p. 2.

24. Quoted in Kenneth J. Atchity, ed., *The Classical Greek Reader*. New York: Oxford University Press, 1996, p. 43.

25. Quoted in Atchity, *The Classical Greek Reader*, p. 288.

26. Pindar, *Odes*, trans. C.M. Bowra. New York: Penguin, 1969, p. 206.

27. Freeman, *The Greek Achievement*, p. 206.

28. Lysias, *Against Eratosthenes*, in *The Murder of Herodes and Other Trials from the Athenian Law Courts*, ed. and trans. Kathleen Freeman. New York: W.W. Norton, 1963, p. 54.

29. Archimedes, *Sand-Reckoner*, quoted in Atchity, *The Classical Greek Reader*, p. 263.

30. Quoted in Atchity, *The Classical Greek Reader*, p. 355.

Chapter 4: Theater and Drama

31. Aristotle, *Poetics*, in *Introduction to Aristotle*, ed. Richard McKeon. New York: Random House, 1947, p. 629.

32. Iris Brook, *Costume in Greek Classic Drama*. London: Methuen, 1962, pp. 76–77.

33. Herodotus, *The Histories*, trans. Aubrey de Sélincourt. New York: Penguin Books, 1972, p. 395.

34. James H. Butler, *The Theater and Drama of Greece and Rome*. San Francisco: Chandler, 1972, pp. 30–31.

35. Paul Roche, introduction to *The Orestes Plays of Aeschylus*, by Aeschylus, trans. Paul Roche. New York: New American Library, 1962, p. xvii.

36. Aeschylus, *Persians*, in *Aeschylus: Prometheus Bound, The Suppliants, Seven Against Thebes, Persians*, trans. Philip Vellacott. Baltimore: Penguin, 1961, pp. 133–34.

37. Sophocles, *Antigone*, lines 368–406, trans. Don Nardo.

Chapter 5: Athletic Competitions

38. See, for example, Plato's *Laws*, in *Plato*, trans. Benjamin Jowett. Chicago: Encyclopaedia Britannica, 1952, p. 670.

39. Vera Olivova, *Sports and Games in the Ancient World*. New York: St. Martin's, 1984, p. 120.

40. Judith Swaddling, *The Ancient Olympic Games*. Austin: University of Texas Press, 1996, p. 12.

41. Quoted in M.I. Finley and H.W. Pleket, *The Olympic Games: The First Thousand Years*. New York: Viking, 1976, p. 27.

42. Pausanius, *Guide to Greece*, vol. 2, p. 272.

43. Pausanius, *Guide to Greece*, vol. 2, p. 236.

44. Plato, *Laws*, in *Plato*, p. 726.

45. Pausanius, *Guide to Greece*, vol. 1, pp. 88–89.

46. Pindar, *Odes*, p. 236.

47. David C. Young, *The Olympic Myth of Greek Amateur Athletics*. Chicago: Ares, 1984, p. 176.

Chapter 6: Leisure Activities and Games

48. Edith Hamilton, *The Greek Way*. New York: W.W. Norton, 1942, p. 18.

49. Hamilton, *The Greek Way*, pp. 18–19.

50. Flaceliere, *Daily Life*, p. 181.

51. Eva Cantarella, *Pandora's Daughters: The Role and Status of Women in Greek and Roman Antiquity*, trans. Maureen B. Fant. Baltimore: Johns Hopkins University Press, 1987, pp. 49–50.

52. Xenophon, *Symposium*, in *Xenophon: Conversations of Socrates*, trans. Hugh Tredennick and Robin Waterfield. New York: Penguin, 1990, pp. 230–32.

53. Waldo E. Sweet, ed., *Sport and Recreation in Ancient Greece: A Sourcebook with Translations*. New York: Oxford University Press, 1987, p. 184.

54. Pindar, *Odes*, pp. 29–30.

55. Aeschylus, *Persians*, p. 134.

56. Lucian, *The Dance*, quoted in Sweet, *Sport and Recreation in Ancient Greece*, pp. 187–88.

57. Homer, *Odyssey*, trans. E.V. Rieu. Baltimore: Penguin, 1961, p. 299.

58. Flaceliere, *Daily Life*, pp. 185–86.

59. Sweet, *Sport and Recreation in Ancient Greece*, p. 155.

60. Quoted in Sweet, *Sport and Recreation in Ancient Greece*, p. 158.

61. Galen, *Exercise with the Small Ball*, in *Selected Works*, trans. P.N. Singer. New York: Oxford University Press, 1997, pp. 299–300.

62. Athenaeus, *Authorities on Banquets*, quoted in J.P.V.D. Balsdon, *Life and Leisure in Ancient Rome*. New York: McGraw-Hill, 1969, p. 164.

63. Julius Pollux, *Thesaurus*, quoted in H.A. Harris, *Sport in Greece and Rome*. Ithaca, NY: Cornell University Press, 1972, p. 86.

64. Homer, *Odyssey*, p. 128.

Glossary

acropolis: "The city's high place"; a hill, usually fortified, central to many Greek towns; the term in upper case (Acropolis) refers to the one in Athens.

agon: A contest or struggle.

agora: A Greek marketplace and/or civic center; the term in uppercase (Agora) refers to the one in Athens.

andron: A room in which the master of a house dined and entertained guests.

aristos: Best.

aulos: A wind instrument today often referred to as a flute, although because it used a reed, it produced a sound more like that of a modern oboe.

black figure: A pottery style in which the painted figures and scenes are black against a reddish orange background. *See* **red figure.**

capital: The decorative top piece of a column.

cella: The main room of a Greek temple, usually housing the cult image (statue) of the god to whom the temple was dedicated.

ceramos: Potter's clay.

choregus (**plural** *choragoi*): A well-to-do backer of plays and other theatrical and cultural events.

colonnade: A row of columns.

cottabos: A party game in which drinkers tried to hit a target with the wine dregs left in their cups.

dithyramb: Ceremonial poetry honoring the fertility god Dionysus; scholars believe that Greek drama developed in part from dithyrambic rituals.

drum: One of several circular stone sections making up a column's shaft.

eccyclema: "Tableau machine"; in the theater, a movable platform on which actors posed in frozen tableaus.

ekechiria: The Olympic truce, during which Greek states were forbidden to make war or impose the death penalty.

entablature: In a Greek-style temple, the structural and usually highly ornamented layer resting between the column tops and the roof.

epinikia: Victory odes; poems written to honor the winners of athletic and other contests; for example, the Olympian, Nemean, Pythian, and Isthmian odes of Pindar.

episkyros: A team ball game probably similar to modern rugby (which is itself a precursor of American football).

fresco: A painting done on wet plaster.

frieze: A painted and/or sculpted ornamental band running around the perimeter of a building, most often a temple.

Geometric: A Greek artistic style (and period) characterized by pottery painted with geometric shapes.

Gigantomachy: The mythical battle between the Olympian gods and a race of monstrous giants.

hetairai (**singular** *hetaira*): "Companions"; high-class prostitutes; educated women who provided men with sex and intelligent conversation.

kalokagathia: A healthy balance between mental (or moral) and physical excellence.

kithara: A large stringed instrument played while standing.

koine: Common tongue or dialect; more specifically, the dialect of Greek (based on the Attic dialect) that became common throughout Greece and the Near East during the Hellenistic Age.

kore (**plural** *korai*): "Young maiden"; often used to describe a female statue whose style was popular in the Archaic Age.

kouros (**plural** *kouroi*): "Youth"; often used to describe a nude male statue whose style was popular in the Archaic Age.

logographai (**singular** *logograhos*): Professional speechwriters, often for litigants in a court case.

lyre (*lyra*): A small harp.

machina: In the theater, a crane or mechanical arm used to "fly" an actor playing a god or hero through the air above the stage.

megaron: In Bronze Age Minoan and Mycenaean palaces, a large hall, usually with a central hearth; later, a kind of house, usually with a columned front porch, a long main room, and a rear storeroom.

oracle: A message thought to come from the gods; or the sacred site where such a message was given; or the priestess who delivered the message.

orchestra: In a Greek theater, the circular stone "dancing" area in which the actors performed.

order: An architectural style, usually identified by the main features of its columns. Columns in the Doric order have no decorative bases, and their capitals are topped by plain rectangular slabs. Columns in the Ionic order *do* have decorative bases, and their capitals are topped by ornamental scrolls.

Orientalizing: A Greek artistic style (and period) characterized by stylistic influences from the Near East.

paean: A hymn or patriotic song.

palaestra: A wrestling school or facility, or a part of a gymnasium devoted to wrestling.

Panathenaea: Athens's largest and most important religious festival, held in August each year but with special splendor (the Greater Panathenaea) every fourth year.

panhellenic: "All-Greek"; used to describe ideas or events common to many or all Greek city-states.

pankration: A rough-and-tumble athletic event that combined elements of wrestling, boxing, and street fighting.

parodoi: Side entrances of a Greek theater.

pediment: A triangular gable at the top of the front or back of a Greek-style temple.

Pentelic marble: A variety of marble having a fine, uniform grain and a dazzling white sheen when viewed in direct sunlight; it is quarried on Mt. Pentelikon, about ten miles northeast of Athens.

periodos: "Period" or "Circuit"; the "big four" athletic games of ancient Greece, including those held at Olympia, Isthmia, Delphi, and Nemea.

phaininda: A ball-playing team sport that may have been similar to modern rugby and other kinds of football.

philhellenism: Admiration for ancient Greek culture.

physis: Nature; or an underlying natural principle; or natural law.

point: A pointed metal tool used by masons and sculptors to alter and carve stone surfaces.

red figure: A pottery style in which the painted figures and scenes are reddish orange against a black background.

rhapsodia: Recitation contests, most often of the Homeric epics.

rhapsodes: Professional poetry reciters, most often of Homer's works.

sanctuary: A sacred area made up of a temple and its surrounding grounds.

skene: "Scene building"; a structure facing the audience area in a Greek theater, containing dressing rooms for the actors.

stoa: A roofed public building, usually long with an open colonnade along one side.

symposium: An after-dinner drinking party, usually in a private home.

terra-cotta: Baked clay.

theatron: The audience or seating area of a Greek theater.

tholos: A conical "beehive" tomb commonly built to house deceased Bronze Age Mycenaean royalty.

For Further Reading

Books

Peter Connolly, *The Legend of Odysseus.* New York: Oxford University Press, 1986. Superbly retells Homer's epics, the *Iliad* and the *Odyssey,* for young readers, aided by numerous beautiful color drawings.

Susie Hodge, *Ancient Greek Art.* Crystal Lake, IL: Heinemann Library, 1998. A very colorfully illustrated guide to Greek arts aimed at young readers.

Robert B. Kebric, *Greek People.* Mountain View, CA: Mayfield, 2001. A superb overview of major ancient Greek figures from all walks of life. The reading level is challenging for students below high school level, but it is well worth the effort.

Don Nardo, *Greek Temples.* New York: Franklin Watts, 2002. A colorfully illustrated overview of how Greek temples were built and used. Written for younger readers.

Don Nardo, ed., *Greek Drama.* San Diego: Greenhaven, 2000. A collection of essays by noted experts about ancient Greek playwrights and their works.

Internet Sources

Hellenic Museum and Cultural Center, "A Day in the Life of an Ancient Greek," www.hellenicmuseum.org. A useful, easy-to-read general source for ancient Greek life, including clothes, food, sports, art, and more.

Tufts University Department of the Classics, "Perseus Project," www.perseus. tufts.edu. The most comprehensive online source about ancient Greece, with hundreds of links to all aspects of Greek history, life, and culture, supported by numerous photos of artifacts.

University of Colorado, "Greek Architecture," http://harpy.uccs.edu. A general overview of ancient Greek architecture, with links to sites about various styles and periods.

Works Consulted

Major Works

Manolis Andronicos, *The Acropolis.* Athens: Ekdotike Athenon, 1994. An excellent overview of the history and features of the famous structures atop Athens's central hill.

William R. Biers, *The Archaeology of Greece.* Ithaca, NY: Cornell University Press, 1996. One of the best general presentations of Greek archaeological artifacts available.

Carl Bluemel, *Greek Sculptors at Work.* London: Phaidon, 1969. Provides detailed information about the tools and methods of ancient Greek sculptors and stonemasons.

John Boardman, *Greek Art.* New York: Praeger, 1964. A classic overview of ancient Greek arts and crafts.

James H. Butler, *The Theater and Drama of Greece and Rome.* San Francisco: Chandler, 1972. Contains all the major pertinent information about ancient Greco-Roman theaters and stagecraft.

Robert M. Cook, *Greek Painted Pottery.* London: Routledge, 1997. The latest edition of Cook's massive and highly informative study of ancient Greek pottery painting, with numerous helpful illustrations.

M.I. Finley and H.W. Pleket, *The Olympic Games: The First Thousand Years.* New York: Viking, 1976. This is a sturdy synopsis of the ancient Olympics, covering the festival, the athletic program, the rules and officials, the athletes, the events, and the spectators.

Peter Green, *The Parthenon.* New York: Newsweek Book Division, 1973. One of the more respected modern classical scholars focuses on the Parthenon while summarizing Athens's golden age.

Ian Jenkins, *The Parthenon Frieze.* Austin: University of Texas, 1994. A thorough study of the Parthenon's Ionic frieze, with numerous helpful photos and diagrams.

John G. Landels, *Music in Ancient Greece and Rome.* London: Routledge, 1998. One of the best of several recent studies on an often neglected topic. The scholarly style will be challenging to the general reader.

A.W. Lawrence, *Greek Architecture.* Rev. R.A. Tomlinson. New Haven, CT: Yale University Press, 1996. A terrific general overview of Greece's ancient structures, their features, artistic styles, uses, and so on.

Peter Levi, *A History of Greek Literature.* New York: Viking, 1985. A very thorough study of the writings of ancient Greece.

Vera Olivova, *Sports and Games in the Ancient World*. New York: St. Martin's, 1984. A thoughtful, informative study of the subject.

John G. Pedley, *Greek Art and Archaeology*. New York: Harry N. Abrams, 1993. A very informative discussion of ancient Greek art and surviving examples.

Nigel Spivey, *Greek Art*. London: Phaidon, 1997. Tells the history of Greek art, touching on mythology, religion, drama, changes in the Hellenistic period, and the legacy of Greek artistic endeavors.

R.E. Wycherly, *The Stones of Athens*. Princeton, NJ: Princeton University Press, 1978. A superior presentation of the archaeological remains of the greatest city of ancient Greece.

Other Important Works

Primary Sources

Aeschylus, *Aeschylus: Prometheus Bound, The Suppliants, Seven Against Thebes, The Persians*. Trans. Philip Vellacott. Baltimore: Penguin, 1961.

———, *Oresteia* trilogy, published as *The Orestes Plays of Aeschylus*. Trans. Paul Roche. New York: New American Library, 1962.

Aristotle, assorted works in *Introduction to Aristotle*. Ed. Richard McKeon. New York: Random House, 1947.

Kenneth J. Atchity, ed., *The Classical Greek Reader*. New York: Oxford University Press, 1996.

Josephine Balmer, trans. *Sappho: Poems and Fragments*. Secaucus, NJ: Meadowland, 1984.

Demosthenes, *Olynthiacs, Philippics, Minor Speeches*. Trans. J.H. Vince. Cambridge, MA: Harvard University Press, 1962.

Euripides, assorted plays in *Euripides: Medea and Other Plays*. Trans. Philip Vellacott. New York: Penguin, 1963.

Kathleen Freeman, ed. and trans., *The Murder of Herodes and Other Trials from the Athenian Law Courts*. New York: W.W. Norton, 1963.

Galen, *Selected Works*. Trans. P.N. Singer. New York: Oxford University Press, 1997.

Herodotus, *The Histories*. Trans. Aubrey de Sélincourt. New York: Penguin Books, 1972.

Homer, *Iliad*. Trans. Robert Fagles. New York: Penguin, 1990.

———, *Odyssey*. Trans. E.V. Rieu. Baltimore: Penguin, 1961.

Pausanias, *Guide to Greece*. 2 vols. Trans. Peter Levi. New York: Penguin, 1971.

Pindar, *Odes*. Trans. C.M. Bowra. New York: Penguin, 1969.

Plato, dialogues and other works in *Plato*. Trans. Benjamin Jowett. Chicago: Encyclopaedia Britannica, 1952.

Plutarch, *Parallel Lives*, excerpted in *The Rise and Fall of Athens: Nine Greek Lives by Plutarch*. Trans. Ian Scott-Kilvert. New York: Penguin, 1960.

J.J. Pollitt, ed. and trans., *The Art of Ancient Greece: Sources and Documents*. New York: Cambridge University Press, 1990.

Waldo E. Sweet, ed., *Sport and Recreation in Ancient Greece: A Sourcebook with Translations*. New York: Oxford University Press, 1987.

Thucydides, *The Peloponnesian War*. Trans. Rex Warner. New York: Penguin, 1972.

Xenophon, *Symposium*, in *Xenophon: Conversations of Socrates*. Trans. Hugh Tredennick and Robin Waterfield. New York: Penguin, 1990.

Modern Sources

Lesley Adkins and Roy A. Adkins, *Handbook to Life in Ancient Greece*. New York: Facts On File, 1997.

J.P.V.D. Balsdon, *Life and Leisure in Ancient Rome*. New York: McGraw-Hill, 1969.

John Boardman, *Athenian Black Figure Vases*. New York: Oxford University Press, 1974.

———, *Athenian Red Figure Vases: The Classical Period, a Handbook*. London: Thames and Hudson, 1989.

———, *Greek Sculpture: The Archaic Age*. London: Thames and Hudson, 1978.

C.M. Bowra, *Ancient Greek Literature*. New York: Oxford University Press, 1960.

Iris Brook, *Costume in Greek Classic Drama*. London: Methuen, 1962.

Eva Cantarella, *Pandora's Daughters: The Role and Status of Women in Greek and Roman Antiquity*. Trans. Maureen B. Fant. Baltimore: Johns Hopkins University Press, 1987.

Lionel Casson, *Masters of Ancient Comedy*. New York: Macmillan, 1960.

Richard Clogg, *A Concise History of Greece*. New York: Cambridge University Press, 1992.

J.J. Coulton, *Ancient Greek Architects at Work*. Ithaca, NY: Cornell University Press, 1977.

Thomas Craven, *The Pocket Book of Greek Art*. New York: Pocket, 1950.

Robert Flaceliere, *Daily Life in Greece at the Time of Pericles*. Trans. Peter Green. London: Phoenix, 1996.

———, *A Literary History of Greece*. Trans. Douglas Garman. Chicago: Aldine, 1964.

Charles Freeman, *The Greek Achievement: The Foundation of the Western World*. New York: Viking, 1999.

Edith Hamilton, *The Greek Way*. New York: W.W. Norton, 1942.

H.A. Harris, *Sport in Greece and Rome*. Ithaca, NY: Cornell University Press, 1972.

Thomas R. Martin, *Ancient Greece: From Prehistoric to Hellenistic Times*. New Haven, CT: Yale University Press, 1996.

Jennifer Neils, *Goddess and Polis: The Panathenaic Festival in Ancient Athens*. Princeton, NJ: Princeton University Press, 1992.

Michael B. Poliakoff, *Combat Sports in the Ancient World*. New Haven, CT: Yale University Press, 1987.

Sarah B. Pomeroy et al., *Ancient Greece: A Political, Social, and Cultural History*. New York: Oxford University Press, 1999.

Chester G. Starr, *The Ancient Greeks*. New York: Oxford University Press, 1971.

———, *A History of the Ancient World*. New York: Oxford University Press, 1991.

Judith Swaddling, *The Ancient Olympic Games*. Austin: University of Texas Press, 1996.

David C. Young, *The Olympic Myth of Greek Amateur Athletics*. Chicago: Ares, 1984.

Index

Picture Credits

About the Author

Historian Don Nardo has written and edited numerous volumes about the ancient Greek world, including *Greek and Roman Sport, The Age of Pericles, The Parthenon, Life in Ancient Athens, The Decline and Fall of Ancient Greece,* and literary companions to the works of Homer, Euripides, and Sophocles. He resides with his wife, Christine, in Massachusetts.